T0381171

# Mastering Technical Art
# in Unreal Engine

This book covers how to use the latest development tools to create your own Virtual World powered by Unreal Engine. Each chapter will provide you with the necessary underpinning theory as well as activities to test your learning inside of Unreal Engine.

You'll learn about Landscapes, Sculpting, Materials, Foliage, Water, Partitions and much more as you complete project-based examples. Included in the book is a series of follow-along introductory videos and quizzes to help test your learning, giving you all the tools and knowledge to make detailed believable worlds in Unreal Engine.

This book will be of great interest to all students learning to create technical art within Unreal Engine, as well as professionals looking to sharpen their skills.

# Mastering Technical Art in Unreal Engine
## World Building

Greg Penninck and Stuart Butler

CRC Press
Taylor & Francis Group
Boca Raton   London   New York

CRC Press is an imprint of the
Taylor & Francis Group, an **informa** business

Designed cover image: Greg Penninck and Stuart Butler

First edition published 2025
by CRC Press
2385 NW Executive Center Drive, Suite 320, Boca Raton FL 33431

and by CRC Press
4 Park Square, Milton Park, Abingdon, Oxon, OX14 4RN

*CRC Press is an imprint of Taylor & Francis Group, LLC*

© 2025 Greg Penninck and Stuart Butler

ISBN: 978-1-032-66387-6 (hbk)
ISBN: 978-1-032-64973-3 (pbk)
ISBN: 978-1-032-66388-3 (ebk)
ISBN: 978-1-032-66390-6 (eBook+)

DOI: 10.1201/9781032663883

Typeset in Times
by codeMantra

Access the support material: http://www.routledge.com/9781032649733

*This book series is dedicated to the love of creating real-time artwork for Unreal Engine. The joy of working on games and being involved in the community of creation is only superseded by the feeling of seeing your content in a shipped product being enjoyed by millions of gamers. Unreal Engine has brought such joy to the game development community, and this series aims to bring a chunk of joy to the next generation of developers, hobbyists and creators.*

*In addition, the books are dedicated to the many students, team members and educators who we have had the pleasure to work with. Your passion and love for the creation of games is inspirational and encourage us to push our own work to higher levels. We'd also like to make a special shout-out to the students who studied online with us during the pandemic, who no doubt have long-lasting memories of Stu's "questions".*

*To my partner, Liz, for her incredible patience, support and energy as I burnt many a midnight hour developing Unreal content and muttered strange phrases like "shaders are compiling". To my children, Tasha and Thomas, for their enthusiasm and interest in the Unreal Engine and Games. – Greg Penninck*

*To my wife, Becky, for her continued support and tolerance of me continuing along this journey (even while editing on our holiday in the woods) in the pursuit of professional growth and success. To my boys, Jack, Zach and Lincoln, for their understanding and continued excitement of me writing another book. – Stuart Butler*

# Contents

Preface ................................................................................................................ xi
Acknowledgments ............................................................................................. xiii
Author Biographies ........................................................................................... xiv

**1. What Is World Building** ................................................................................. 1
   What Is World Building? ................................................................................. 1
   Resources and Ingredients for World Building ............................................. 1
      One Sheet Concepts ................................................................................. 1
      Project Goals ............................................................................................ 2
      Reference Acquisition ............................................................................. 2
   Unreal World Building Pipeline ..................................................................... 3
      Actors ....................................................................................................... 3
      Level ......................................................................................................... 5
      Experience ................................................................................................ 6
   Getting Started with the Project Files ............................................................. 8
      Installing Unreal Engine .......................................................................... 8
      Extracting the Project ............................................................................... 8
      Opening the Project ................................................................................. 9
   Starting Our Unreal Level .............................................................................. 9
      Setting up Level Streaming ...................................................................... 10
      World Outliner Conventions ................................................................... 11
   Conclusion ...................................................................................................... 12
   Chapter 1 Quiz ............................................................................................... 13
      Answers .................................................................................................... 13

**2. Blocking Out in Unreal** ................................................................................. 14
   Why Block Out ............................................................................................... 14
   Tools for Blocking Out in Unreal ................................................................... 14
   The Unreal Engine Viewport .......................................................................... 16
   Exploring the Tools ........................................................................................ 16
      Blocking Out the Main Tower ................................................................. 16
      Adding the Embattlements with CubeGrid ............................................ 20
      Adding Stairs to the Block Out ............................................................... 22
      Adding the Chimney ............................................................................... 25
   Reusing a Block Out ....................................................................................... 26
      Packed Level Actors ................................................................................ 26
      Merged Actor ........................................................................................... 27
   Conclusion ...................................................................................................... 27
   Chapter 2 Quiz ............................................................................................... 27
      Answers .................................................................................................... 28

3. **Introduction to Unreal Landscapes**..............................................................29
   Introduction to Landscapes .................................................................29
   Common Approaches to Landscape Creation........................................29
   Starting a New Landscape .....................................................................30
   Working with Landscape Mode .............................................................31
   Using Landscape Sculpting Tools ..........................................................32
   Using Landscape Heightmaps.................................................................36
   Conclusion ...............................................................................................38
   Chapter 3  Quiz .......................................................................................39
     Answers ...............................................................................................39

4. **Introduction to Unreal Landscape Materials**..........................................40
   Introduction to Landscape Materials .....................................................40
   Landscape Material Requirements .........................................................40
   Creating Our First Landscape Material ..................................................41
   Applying and Painting Our First Landscape Material............................43
   Material Functions for Landscape Layers...............................................46
     Ingredients for Our Landscape Layer Material Function .................47
     Building Our Landscape Layer Material Function .............................47
   Conclusion ...............................................................................................56
   Chapter 4  Quiz .......................................................................................56
     Answers ...............................................................................................57

5. **Creating Layered Landscape Materials** ....................................................58
   Introduction to Layered Landscape Materials .......................................58
   Using Material Functions to Create Landscape Layers ..........................58
     Adding Our Material Function ..........................................................58
     Creating Mud, Grass, Stone and River Mud.....................................60
   Blending Landscape Layers ....................................................................68
     Controlling Specularity......................................................................68
   Runtime Virtual Texturing for Landscapes ...........................................72
     Setting up Our RVT Material Links ..................................................72
     Setting up Virtual Texture Volumes and Drawing Virtual Textures..........75
   Setting up Tiling and Fading Controls...................................................79
   Conclusion ...............................................................................................85
   Chapter 5  Quiz .......................................................................................87
     Answers ...............................................................................................87

6. **Foliage**..........................................................................................................88
   Introduction to Unreal Foliage Tools ....................................................88
   Creating Our First Foliage Asset ...........................................................89
   Painting Foliage Assets ..........................................................................91
   Setting Up Our Static Mesh Foliage ......................................................94
   Creating Our Procedural Foliage Spawner ............................................96
   Conclusion ............................................................................................. 100
   Chapter 6  Quiz ..................................................................................... 101
     Answers............................................................................................. 101

**7. Water** ................................................................................ 102
  Introduction to Unreal Water Tools ........................................... 102
  Enabling the Water Plugins ...................................................... 102
  Water Body Actors ................................................................... 103
    Setting Up Water Body Ocean Actors ................................... 104
    Water Body River Actors ..................................................... 108
    Setting Up Water Body Lake Actors ...................................... 111
    Setting Up Extra River Actors .............................................. 113
    Experimenting with Curl Noise ............................................. 114
    Further Customization .......................................................... 114
  Conclusion ............................................................................. 117
  Chapter 7 Quiz ...................................................................... 118
    Answers ............................................................................... 118

**8. Landmass Tools** ................................................................. 119
  Introduction to Landscape Materials ......................................... 119
  Creating Your First Landmass Brush ......................................... 120
  Exploring the Landmass Brush Details Panel ............................. 121
  Creating Our Second Landmass Brush ....................................... 124
  Creating a Landmass Material Brush ......................................... 125
  Conclusion ............................................................................. 128
  Chapter 8 Quiz ...................................................................... 128
    Answers ............................................................................... 129

**9. Introduction to Procedural World Decoration** ..................... 130
  Introduction to Procedural World Decoration ............................. 130
    Procedural Content Graph .................................................... 130
    PCG Actors .......................................................................... 131
    Debugging PCG Attributes .................................................... 132
  Tree and Rock Spawner ........................................................... 133
  Grass Spawner ....................................................................... 139
  Pumpkin Spawner ................................................................... 141
  Conclusion ............................................................................. 147
  Chapter 9 Quiz ...................................................................... 147
    Answers ............................................................................... 148

**10. Auto Landscape Materials** ............................................... 149
  Auto Landscape Materials ....................................................... 149
  Masking Height ...................................................................... 150
  Masking Slopes ...................................................................... 150
  Blending Setup for Rock and Stone .......................................... 154
  Blending Setup for Grass ........................................................ 156
  Connecting It to Our Existing Landscape Material ..................... 156
  Corrective Painting ................................................................. 161
  Conclusion ............................................................................. 163
  Chapter 10 Quiz .................................................................... 163
    Answers ............................................................................... 164

**11. World Partition**............................................................................................ 165
    What Is World Partition?................................................................................ 165
    Exploring World Partition ............................................................................. 165
        The World Partition Editor........................................................................ 166
        World Partition in Action ......................................................................... 168
        Working with Multiple Grids .................................................................... 171
    Using World Partition on an Existing Level ..................................................... 172
    Using Data Layers ......................................................................................... 174
    Conclusion ................................................................................................... 175
    Chapter 11  Quiz........................................................................................... 175
        Answers ................................................................................................. 176

**12. Lighting and Environment Effects** ............................................................. 177
    Introduction to Lighting and Environment Effects............................................ 177
    Lighting Systems and Mobility ....................................................................... 177
        UE5  Lightmass...................................................................................... 177
        UE5  Path Tracer .................................................................................... 178
        UE5  Lumen ........................................................................................... 178
    Unreal Light Types........................................................................................ 179
        Light Mobility ........................................................................................ 180
        Light Properties...................................................................................... 180
    Physical versus Artistic Units ........................................................................ 182
    Environment Light Mixer ............................................................................... 183
    Post Processing............................................................................................. 183
    Lighting Exercise One: Let There Be DayLight ............................................... 186
        Lighting a Cloudy Midday Exterior............................................................ 186
    Lighting Exercises Two: Golden Hour............................................................. 194
    Lighting Exercises Three: Nighttime............................................................... 196
    Screenshots and Capturing Your Work............................................................204
    Conclusion ...................................................................................................208
    Chapter 12  Quiz ..........................................................................................208
        Answers .................................................................................................209

**Index**........................................................................................................... 211

# *Preface*

## Introduction to the Series

Welcome to this book series: *Mastering Technical Art in Unreal Engine*. In this second book, we will be exploring World Building and creating exciting Technical Art content and systems directly in Unreal Engine 5. You will begin by working with Unreal Engine Blockout and Landscape Tools, learning how to create detailed Landscapes eventually realizing an entire world with foliage, water, materials, lighting and more.

This book represents over 20 years of teaching and development experience that has helped educate and develop many game artists working in the UK games industry today. We will share straightforward and engaging exercises for you to practice and test yourself against to help you master your Unreal Engine Technical Art skills.

## World Building

In this book, you'll learn the art of creating Real-time landscapes. You'll master both technical and artistic skills to create stunning Real-time worlds that make use of modern engine workflows. Worlds in games now require multiple developers to populate complex ecosystems; with this title, you'll learn how to work with all kinds of different developers and systems to realize Unreal Landscapes.

## Materials and VFX

In our first book, we'll begin by creating Game Materials to help render 3D Models. You'll develop skills that allow you to create optimized materials and explore ways of creating parameterized Master Materials. You'll then utilize your skills to help create engaging VFX with Niagara learning to create Real-Time particles utilizing materials. This book will give you the introductory skills to begin your mastery journey in the field of Technical Art.

## How to Use This book

There are a couple of things you need to know about this book and how we have presented the activities, in order for you to get the most out of each chapter.

## Reading Step-by-Step Instructions

Each chapter features multiple step-by-step tutorials to guide you through World Building techniques and systems; the following formatting styles have been used, and understanding these will help you speed through each activity with ease:

- **Bold Text** – When you see bold text, this is something to look out for on screen. These include labels on the user interface, such as the **Details** panel, parameters such as **Sort Priority**, names of nodes such as **Multiply (0,1)** and many more.
- *Italic Text* – When you see italic text, this is something for you to enter by typing, such as *Diffuse Texture* when renaming nodes, values to enter such as *1.25*, something to search for in a search box such as *OneMinus* or something to select from a dropdown.

As we go through the book, we will provide parameter values in tutorials. Many of these can be adjusted to achieve different end results, and we encourage you to play with these values to see what they do and how changing them affects the end result; don't worry if your final result isn't 100% perfect, that is all part of the process of learning Technical Art.

## Unreal Engine Version

The tutorials in this book have been created using Unreal Engine version 5.3. If you don't already have this installed on your computer, there is a quick guide included in Chapter 1.

## Project Files

At the start of Chapter 1, we will also ask you to download some project files we have created for you to use throughout the book. When using these, it's a good idea to keep a copy of the original levels, just in case, you want to jump back to start again without needing to create a whole new project.

## Practice, Practice, Practice!

Many of the tools and techniques we discuss in this book may feel complex, confusing and sometimes challenging when you first start out. Don't worry! Over time, as Unreal and it's many tools become more familiar, the processes themselves will become second nature as you develop a deeper understanding of the engine and its various editors.

## Crashes!

Games Engines are continually evolving software which are always in development; so they will often suffer from crashes, errors and other issues that may feel frustrating. Don't worry, it happens to all of us and it's rarely something you will have done.

For that reason, we will often prompt you to save your work, while Unreal does have an Autosave, it's always worth manually saving each time you create/refine or finish an asset so when the inevitable does happen, you can simply restart the software, reload the project and level and continue where you left off.

# *Acknowledgments*

I would like to thank my family and colleagues for their time and love during the creation of this book. I'd also like to thank Bobbie Fletcher, Nader Alikhani and Cris Robson for their guidance and support during the early parts of my career. Lastly, I'd like to thank Stu for coping with the severe level of Gregisms and nonsense throughout our books and beyond. – Greg Penninck

I would like to thank my family for their endless amounts of support and my colleagues, both old and new, for their words of guidance and support. I'd also like to thank Bobbie Fletcher for affording me many professional opportunities and for always being a great mentor and Justin Mohlman for giving me my first opportunity to develop educational content for an international audience. Lastly, I'd also like to thank Greg, one of the most talented and knowledgeable individuals I've had the pleasure of working with, for sharing this journey of authoring with me. – Stuart Butler

# *Author Biographies*

**Greg Penninck** has worked and taught in the Games Industry sector since 2006, creating many world-leading games courses and modules from Foundation to Masters Level. He is an Authorized Unreal Instructor Partner for Epic Games and has been teaching Unreal Engine for over 15 years. In 2016, he was awarded an Epic Developer Grant through his company Thundersteed Ltd., which helped him continue to spread the joy of Unreal Development. He works as a Marketing Artist for REALTIME, a BAFTA-nominated VFX Studio.

**Stuart Butler** is the Dean of Creative Industries at CG Spectrum Institute. He has taught in the HE sector since 2009, creating many games courses and modules from Foundation to Masters Level, and he was formerly the Course Director of Games Technology at Staffordshire University. He is an Authorized Unreal Instructor Partner and Educational Content Creator for Epic Games, and he has been teaching Unreal Engine since the launch of UDK. He has contributed to projects as a Vehicle Artist, Animator, Game Designer and Technical Designer/Artist; his broad skillset and understanding provide insight into all aspects of Games Development. Alongside Greg, as part of their Company Thundersteed Ltd., he was awarded an Epic Developer Grant in 2016.

# 1

## What Is World Building

## What Is World Building?

No matter your project's target, Unreal offers a supreme toolset for creating beautiful interactive worlds. World Building is the process of creating these wonderful worlds, and this book will guide you through the various designs, technical and creative tool sets that will help you realize your ideas.

To get started, we first need to explore Epic's overall World Building pipeline and more importantly, what resources we might need to get started.

## Resources and Ingredients for World Building

To begin a World Building project, you should gather and collate a large amount of references, inspiration and design-related material to help you answer questions about your world. There are many questions you could ask, but starting simple helps you work fast.

### One Sheet Concepts

A simple conceptual starting point could be a one sheet/page design that focuses on the following questions:

### What?

- What is your world's name?
- What would a one-sentence summary of the project contain?
- What is the main focus of your world?
- What are the key objects of your world?

### Where Is Your World?

- What is the climate like?
- What type of landscape or terrain is it situated in?
- What time of day is it?
- What is the general mood/ambience?

DOI: 10.1201/9781032663883-1

## Why?

- Is there an embedded story in the world?
- Is your world a specific setting that ties many things together, for example, a factory?
- Is there a certain emotion/feeling you want to evoke in the viewer/player?

## How?

- Is it obvious how the viewer/player arrived in the world?
- Was there any drama/ongoing event in the world?

After answering broad questions that address things like locale or overarching ideas, you could then explore more technical elements that may require research or even goals that you wish to explore to push your skills further. Let's explore a couple of these:

## Project Goals

- How does your world work? Is it a playable game level/cinematic/still imagery?
- Are there skills you'd wish to develop? For example, procedurally generated foliage/scenery.
- Are there asset packs you might wish to include? For example, Megascans Nordic Assets.

With your goals and concepts in mind, you can then start to build up a library of reference and research material. There is no real limit as to what you could or should collect, but you should ensure your imagery and research material is easily accessible throughout your project and helps to answer questions. There are many modern tools that can help you contain image-based references such as PureRef, Miro, Pinterest and Wiki's. A folder on a hard drive is always going to be the default starting place, but these websites and tools will help elevate your ability to compare your progress, particularly if you have a second monitor.

## Reference Acquisition

The last thing to determine is what should the focus of the references we gather be? There are many areas that may help and, depending on the project, what you need will change, but the list below is a good starting point for any project.

- Setting and location
- Props and objects
- Color and texture
- Shape and visual language
- Audio samples

- VFX textures/animations
- Lighting
- Layout sketches, focal point sketches, and blockout
- Technical approaches and tutorials

## Unreal World Building Pipeline

Epic's World Building Pipeline consists of three main sections: Actors, Level and Experience. Within each of these sections, there are multiple ingredients and functionality that can be added to our worlds.

Let's explore the three areas independently to see what they might mean to our process.

### Actors

Actors are entities that can be placed inside of a level. There are many types of Actor, Epic group them into Meshes and None Mesh Actors. The idea here is that we place Meshes in our Game Worlds to help decorate or create the structure of scenery, whereas a None Mesh Actor might add features such as lighting or audio to our environments.

### *Mesh Actors*

Mesh Actors contain some form of 3D geometry, they build up the bulk of the visual appearance of our worlds. It's important that our Mesh actors are built well prior to their use in Unreal, this means lengthy discussions with art terms to ensure best practices are used in digital content creation (DCC) tools when building assets. What are the different types we might come across?

- **Static Meshes** – These are 3D models that do not move; for landscape decoration, this might include things like buildings, rocks, signage and other types of decoration.
- **Skeletal Meshes** – These are 3D models which have a rig/skeleton assigned to them. They are used primarily for characters but for landscape decoration we might also use them for flags, chains, and complex physics animations.
- **Spline Meshes** – These are actors which are made up of repeating mesh parts. A basic example of Spline Meshes would be a cylinder mesh used to represent models such as ropes and cables, however, more complicated meshes can be used for many Spline Mesh systems such as fences and even roads.
- **Hierarchical Level of Detail** – Hierarchical level of details (HLODs) are groups of distance meshes. In Unreal, we can group distance models together and create a proxy mesh to help improve rendering performance.
- **Instances** – There are a variety of systems in Unreal that aim to improve rendering by Instancing Meshes. These are often Procedural Content Graphs

and or Foliage Rendering where we might want to render several thousand copies of the exact same mesh.

- **Dynamic Meshes** – Unreal also provides many options for procedurally spawning and customizing meshes. Allowing the users to take meshes from DCCs and build on top of them. For example, covering a cliff face with snow. While this side of creation in Unreal is a more modern workflow expect to see proceduralism grow in Unreal over the coming versions.

## None Mesh Actors

None Mesh Actors usually add functionality to our worlds in some way or another. They can still include meshes, but their primary goal is usually functionality. For example, a Character Blueprint may include a Character Mesh, but it will also be accompanied by a lot of logic and systems. None Mesh Actors come in a wide variety of types and are often added later in the pipeline to help finesse or polish a world. Let's now explore some key types.

- **Lights** – There is a wide variety of Light Actors which we'll explore later in the book. They contribute to the illumination scene and can be heavily customized to create the mood and feeling required in our world.
- **Emitters** – This is the term often used to describe Particle Effects. In UE5, VFX is controlled by Niagara Systems that spawn and play Niagara Emitters within our Levels. If you are interested in learning more about Niagara you could always look up our first book, Mastering Technical Art in Unreal Engine – Materials and VFX.
- **Audio** – Actors such as Ambient Sound actors can be used to control the world-related background VFX or even music. Event/specific audio tracks are embedded in Blueprints or used in combination with other systems such as Unreals Cinematic Tool Sequencer.
- **Volumes** – These are actors that carry out a specific function when a player or camera is inside of a space. They are used for all kinds of things such as triggering events, changing camera colors or even altering the state of physics within a game.
- **Gameplay/Other Blueprints** – Blueprints are used for many things inside of World Building projects and are a big component of Unreal Engine. They carry out specific functionality that a Developer has created. We could use Blueprints for placing trees, rendering clouds, pickups, level objectives or triggering Emitter VFX.

## Placeable World Building Actors

- **Foliage** – We are able to create Foliage in a number of ways in Unreal, we can use a special Foliage mode to paint Instanced Foliage Actors, we can use Procedural Foliage Volumes, and we can use Procedural Content Graphs to spawn meshes. Scope and scale often dictate some form of proceduralism, whereas the Foliage mode is more creative.

- **Landscapes** – Landscape Actors control the appearance and functionality of our World's Landscape. We'll be utilizing the systems and tools in the Editor across several chapters to develop Landscape shapes, materials and foliage.
- **Water** – Unreal has several experimental Water Actors that can replicate different types of water bodies, for example, Oceans and Rivers. These bodies also merge nicely with the Landscape tools, allowing the water to deform Landscape Actors.

## Level

Level Actors/Systems control functionality that occurs within a designated level. In some cases, the systems may only work in one intended level, and in others, they may carry over multiple levels. It's important in a game development scenario to plan out features that can be utilized in several circumstances rather than creating bespoke systems each time. We'll begin by exploring how levels are set up and how data is stored in Editor systems such as the World Outliner in this Chapter.

- **Sequencer** – Sequencer Assets provide us with an opportunity to construct in game cinematics. This is a great way to showcase our World Building projects. Sequencer Assets are constructed in Sequencer and can then be played within a level. In the games you love and play, this may be something as simple as a camera reveal or a full cinematic.
- **Variant Manager** – The Variant Manager is a specialized editor that allows us to set up pre-configurations of actors. It's particularly useful for configurators where we might want a car or an item to have several easily predefined presets. For World Building, we can leverage this to set up customizable paint jobs and meshes for all kinds of environmental assets.
- **Level Blueprint** – Levels contain their own Blueprint Editor which allows us to write Blueprint Logic that can execute when a level is loaded or as certain level actors are interacted with. This is particularly helpful if you need a Camera change, a Trigger Event and or a lighting update. In a games pipeline, developers often avoid Level Blueprint as it's easy for gameplay scripting to become disjointed if a game has hundreds of levels. For a World Building project, however you may find it quite useful to activate Blueprint within the Level Blueprint instead of building complex gameplay Blueprints.
- **World Partition/Streaming** – Levels can be set up in a number of ways. As a standalone Level with no other connections or with a version of Level Streaming. The idea of Level Streaming is that depending on where a player or viewer is, assets/other levels are seamlessly blended into Camera. This concept allows Unreal to build huge worlds with seamlessly unlimited detail. We'll explore a couple of variations on this concept as the book progresses.
- **Environment Light Mixer** – Lighting is such an enormously important part of building worlds. The Environment Light Mixer helps us configure the most important actors and systems within a level to effortlessly art direct our scenes. The Mixer is set up to focus on large-scale atmospheric and mood changes, which is great for defining the dominant light direction and themes within a World Building Project.

## Experience

The Unreal Editor provides us with many visual and statistical feedback mechanisms that help us tailor World Building experiences. Sometimes, things go wrong, and Unreal has a plethora of tools that allow us to understand why things might not be working or how we can leverage the engine to improve visual/gameplay performance.

### *Profiling*

Profiling Tools allow us to understand what is happening within the Editor. The options presented to developers vary from simple commands and Editor Panels to full Analytical executables. As a world builder, we are interested in the knock on effect of our choices and need to know what tools we can leverage to better understand how they affect gameplay/visual quality.

- **View Modes** – Unreal's Viewport and Visual Feedback is a massively important part of what makes the software so great. Often referred to as What You See Is What You Get (WYSIWYG) editor. View modes are a key cornerstone of the Viewport and allow us to look at our Levels through different lenses. For example, we can use specific View Modes to evaluate the color pass, roughness pass, detail lighting pass and/or special optimization modes such as Shader Complexity to help debug performance.

- **Scalability** – Scalability options within the Editor, first, allow us to configure the graphic performance of the engine. If a project is too intensive for us to run on a device, we can select a lower scalability which will degrade the visual quality to improve performance and, second, we can use Scalability in combinations with testing to somewhat emulate how a project might run on another device. It's quite possible that you'll need to refer to Unreal's scalability options through this book if your personal computer is not equipped with a modern GPU. To access this menu, click on the Settings Cog Icon near the top right of the Unreal Editor Interface. From the pop-up menu, select Engine Scalability Settings. This menu lets you apply settings to alter performance from Low looking the worst visually but being the fastest to run through to Cinematic, which offers the best graphics but will run the slowest.

- **Statistics Panel** – The Statistics Panel provides us with an easy way to understand what is in our levels. The data are presented in a spreadsheet-like manner with easy column sorting to help you understand where your budgets are being spent. For example, we can review triangle counts across all of our meshes or texture resolution across level actors and the overall level total. Easy access to data makes it simple to optimize and isolate problem meshes/actors.

- **GPU Panel** – Unreal has a variety of tools to help us profile our Graphics Rendering. The GPU Panel is a quick way to see frames broken down into tasks and the time taken to complete. It can be accessed by executing the console command *ProfileGPU*. This is yet another fantastic way to help isolate problem activities when your performance is low. In addition to ProfileGPU, we also have more complex tools within the Unreal Insights application for very precise analytics.

## Building/Rebuilding

Building and Rebuilding in Unreal is the idea of completing a baking process of some sort, the baking process task is often to capture data from our level actors and translate it into data, which can be loaded when the game runs. When rebuilding any part of a level, there is always a chance that some part of your design or work might be misinterpreted or not processed as expected, so it's important to keep an eye on the results that Unreal presents you with.

Let's explore some of the actors that contribute to Unreal's building process, they exist across a number of systems such as navigation, lighting, reflections and more.

- **Nav Meshes** – Nav Meshes are utilized by Unreal's AI actors. While building worlds, we may be required to add in Nav Mesh Volumes, which help the engine understand what Landscapes and Meshes are navigable by AI actors. The result of this process becomes out of date when we alter our level geometry, so expect to see messages and prompts to rebuild it if you are working on a gameplay project.
- **Reflection Captures** – Unreal affords several distinctive rendering workflows. Reflection Capture Actors are somewhat in the process of being phased out as Ray Tracing becomes more commonplace, however, older Hardware still requires Reflection Actors that are placed throughout a level to help generate reflections. Unreal provides several types of these actors, for example, Planar Reflections for Mirrors or Spherical Reflection Capture Actors for general reflections. We are still in a period of time where we may need to place these actors as a fallback, not all consoles are equal and sometimes you may need to develop your world for a low spec device.
- **Lights** – Lighting, in a similar way to reflections, has several conflicting workflows in modern games. It's quite common for developers to use hybrid solutions where some lights are baked and some are not. Unreal provides options for both baked lighting, through Unreal Lightmass, and fully Hardware Ray Tracing via Lumen. Should your world require baked lighting you will need to explore things like Lightmap Resolution and World Settings to ensure your geometry and levels have appropriate quality settings. Baking lighting with higher-quality settings can take several hours, definitely factor in additional time for any baked/built lights.
- **Proxy LODs/HLODs** – Unreal offers several systems for general Level of Detail meshes or LODS. In World Building, the common feature set is called HLOD. HLODs are generated from a selection of background models with the idea of letting Unreal generate a simplified model from a group of many. Processes like this naturally lower the visual fidelity to make a scene run faster. As a World Builder, we can choose what's important, sometimes we might not need to work on a project that needs to run at 60 fps so we might be able to avoid LODs and many baking processes.

## Getting Started with the Project Files

To follow the practical tutorials in this book, you are going to download the project files which are available from the Taylor and Francis website at http://www.routledge.com/9781032649733

You will also need to have Unreal Engine 5.3 installed on your computer.

## Installing Unreal Engine

You can download Unreal Engine via the Epic Games Launcher (available from https://unrealengine.com) in the Unreal Engine section (left-hand side), Library tab. All project files are provided for use in Unreal Engine 5.3, they should work in newer versions (however, some issues may occur) but will not work in any version lower than 5.3. If this is the first time you've installed Unreal Engine, your Epic Launcher after version 5.3 has been installed should look similar to Figure 1.1.

## Extracting the Project

The project download is provided as a .zip archive. This will need extracting (or unzipping) using either the tool built-in to your operating system or with a program such as 7-Zip.

When extracting the project, ensure that you maintain the folder structure and do not move any files around, as this will prevent the Unreal Engine editor from opening the project correctly.

Once extracted, you should have a root directory called **WizardsDesk**, inside of which you should find two directories (**Config** and **Content**) and a **WizardDeskB2. uproject** file.

**FIGURE 1.1**   Epic games launcher with Unreal Engine 5.3 installed as an available engine version.

**FIGURE 1.2**   The WizardsDesk splash screen with shaders compiling.

## Opening the Project

With the project extracted (ensure you are not looking at the files in a compressed folder), double click on the **WizardDeskB2.uproject** file. This will launch the project in the Unreal Engine editor. If you have multiple versions of the engine installed on your computer, you may be greeted with a pop-up asking you to select an engine version. Ensure you select Unreal Engine 5.3 or newer as mentioned earlier.

The first time you open the project (and any time you open it after a driver update), the loading sequence may appear to stall around the 45% region, don't worry, this is the point at which the engine does its first phase of compiling the shaders for the project and this can take a little time, so having to wait is quite normal. You should see the number of shaders still to be compiled in the bottom left of the splash screen after the loaded percentage indicator, as shown in Figure 1.2.

When the project has opened you will see an example level which shows a finished landscape and World. We'll be exploring this project using its examples as you learn the Unreal systems.

Please take as long as you need to review the level and explore the provided files.

## Starting Our Unreal Level

Now that we've explored the World Building pipeline and Opened the provided project, let's begin to explore what approaches we can take to build our Unreal Level. There are several options when beginning our level creation process these are as follows.

1. **Work Within 1 Single Unreal level** – All of the World Building Pipeline occurs within one level. This is particularly useful when tackling a small prototype or level for a low-end platform such as a mobile game.

2. **Utilize Level Streaming** – Create a Master or HUB level that then links to several other levels, often distinct from one another. An example of this would be a level that handles logic or a level that handles lights and atmospherics. This separation of concerns approach is useful as it can allow teams to work on the same world simultaneously and also takes advantage of Unreal's streaming features to load and unload data. This solution has been used for many years, however, it hits limits on larger projects.

3. **Adopt World Partition** – For games that require a very large open world, Unreal now has a solution known as World Partition. It can dynamically stream areas of the level in without having to work with multiple-level files. Developer teams also use Unreal's One File Per Actor or OFPA when utilizing this solution to allow multiple team members to work on the same level. This solution scales well for large areas and large projects.

During this chapter, we'll look at option two, "Utilize Level Streaming" and then explore option three, "Adopt World Partition" later in the book. The first option, "Work Within 1 Single Unreal level," is incredibly simple to get started with, if you do opt for this approach, try to keep a very clear folder structure at all times in your level's World Outliner and expect to use options two or three in a professional setting, such as working in a studio.

## Setting up Level Streaming

Let's get started in Unreal. First, ensure that the project is open by following the instructions earlier in this chapter.

1. Click on the **File Menu**, select **New Level**.
2. From the pop-up menu select **Empty Level**.
3. If you are requested to save any of the provided files at this point, select not to.
4. An **Empty Level** should show with no content in the **Viewport** or **Outliner**. It's preferable to start this way to avoid inheriting any default settings from other provided example levels.
5. In the **Content Browser**, navigate to the folder **Content | Maps.**
6. Right click in the folder and select **New Folder**. Label the Folder *WizardsDesk*.
7. Next double click on the **WizardsDesk** folder, right click in the folder and select **New Folder**. Label the new folder *levels*.
8. We are now going to save our Main/Master level. To do this click on the **File Menu**. Select **Save Current Level As**. Use the Dialog box to navigate to **Content | Maps | WizardsDesk** and set the name of the level to *WizardsDesk_Main*, then click Save.
9. In the **Content Browser**, navigate to the folder **Content | Maps | WizardsDesk | levels**.

10. Right click in the folder and select **Level** from the pop-up menu. Label the level *WizardsDesk_Lighting*. Right click on the Level asset and select Save.

11. Right click again in the folder and select **Level** from the pop-up menu. Label the level *WizardsDesk_Landscape*. Right click on the Level asset and select **Save**.

12. Click on the **Window** Menu and Select **Levels**. This opens the **Levels** Menu.

13. Select both of the **Level** Assets in the Content Browser folder by holding Ctrl+Left Clicking on them. Next drag and drop both of the **Level Assets** into the **Levels Menu**.

14. You'll now see the term **Persistent Level** above both of the newly added Sub Levels. The level that is highlighted blue is the **Current** level. This means it will be the level that any Actors dropped into the **Viewport** or **Outliner** will be located. You can change this by Double Clicking on any of the levels to make them the **Current** level.

15. Select the **WizardsDesk_Landscape** level listed in the **Levels Menu**, then click the **Pencil Icon/Summon Levels Details**. This opens up the **Level Streaming** Information about the level. Set **Initially Loaded** and **Initially Visible** to *True*. This will mean that the level always loads when the Persistent Level does.

16. Close the **Level Details** menu and right click on the **WizardsDesk_Landscape** level in the **Levels Panel**, Select **Change Streaming Method** and set this to *Always Loaded*.

17. Repeat Instruction 15 and 16 for the **WizardsDesk_Lighting** level.

18. Click the **Floppy Disk/Save Icon** in the **Levels Panel** on the **Persistent Level** to Save your changes.

Congratulations! You now have a level with two correctly set up sublevels that can be utilized to store different types of data. In a production environment, this separation of levels is very useful as it allows multiple developers to work on the different parts of the same level. For solo projects, it's still very good practice as it helps keep our work clean and tidy. We'll explore how to utilize other versions of managing your levels as we go through the book.

Let's now review best practice of adding content to our levels and making best use of the World Outliner.

## World Outliner Conventions

The World Outliner inside of an Unreal Level can get very busy and populated. Each time we add a new actor to a level, a link to it will be created in the World Outliner. Overtime, it can become very full. It is quite common to see several thousand Labels within the Outliner. This can make finding or manipulating groups of actors quite tricky. Epic has provided the World Outliner with a Search box, which does help you if you are aware of the name of the item you need to look for, however, we advocate for the sensible use of Folders to help you quickly identify your Actors. For example, you could split your actors into Folder such as the following.

- Blueprints
- Cinematics
- Landscape
- Meshes
- SFX
- VFX

You may also find it helpful to put a folder near the top of the World Outliner which contains Actors that you might want to tweak throughout development. For example, you may wish to tweak the main Directional Light or Post Process Volume to adjust the mood over time. To enable you to do this, you could create a folder called 00_ LookDev, the addition of the 00_ prefix guarantees that it will always sit above other folders. Numbering other folders in a similar manner will allow you to keep things organized in a way that suits you.

When Actors are placed correctly and set up with folders you should also aim to keep a consistent and well-thought-out naming convention. When an Actor is added to the World Outliner, the default behavior is to label the Actor using the Actor type and then the number it, which relates to in the level, for example, PointLight5. This does not really give us much indication of what the light is used for. A better approach might be PointLight_ExteriorCastle_Blue, this still keeps the Actor type but also includes some information as to where it is, and what it's doing.

Another consideration for Actor placement is the Transforms of Location, Rotation and Scale.

Where possible it's preferably to keep Scale consistent, while this is very idealistic, if your world can be built of assets mostly at a scale of 1.0, it keeps the process simplified as you know that systems such as texture resolution and collision should work as planned. You will naturally break this rule however, particularly with objects like foliage and decorative elements that often require scaling to break up repetition, treat it with caution rather than rigidity.

## Conclusion

As we come to the close of this chapter, we have explored what World Building is and introduced pipeline elements for us to explore over the coming chapters. Using the Unreal Editor, we've also created our first empty level and looked at the process of using Sub Levels to help streamline data. We have also explored the necessary planning and ingredients that we should look to do before getting too involved in Unreal Engine.

In the next chapter, we'll explore how we can begin to blockout and test ideas in Unreal, but before we do, let's take a look at a short quiz!

## Chapter 1  Quiz

Question 1: What is World Building?

a. World building is a Level Editor process that builds all light maps within Unreal.

b. World building is the process of creating beautiful and interactive environments within Unreal.

c. World building is a process that the packaging tools compute to create a platform-targeted version of Unreal.

Question 2: What is the benefit of Sub Levels?

a. Sub Levels allow developers to collaborate in the same space by sectioning off a level into various parts.

b. Sub Levels allow artists to section off lower areas of a level.

c. Sub Levels are 100-m squared sections of a level.

Question 3: What are Unreal Actors?

a. An object which can be placed within a level.

b. Objects that are setup only during Sequencer.

c. Special buttons that spawn terrain meshes.

Question 4: Which are important resources to gather prior to starting a World Building Project?

a. Reference.

b. 3D Models.

c. Environment Blueprints.

d. Sound and Music.

e. All of the above.

## Answers

Question 1: b

Question 2: a

Question 3: a

Question 4: e

# 2

## Blocking Out in Unreal

## Why Block Out

When we start projects, we often have a head full of ideas that need to be turned into a head full of answers, as discussed in Chapter 1. When we start working on our 3D world, those inspirations and concepts need to be turned into digital worlds for our players to explore. The first stage of development is typically to begin with a block out.

Block outs are used across games development in all sorts of disciplines; Animators block out key poses to get a sense of how a character may move, character artists block out major forms and muscle groups to develop silhouettes and a sense of character, level designers block out the flow of a level in a process often referred to as gray boxing, where primitive geometry and gameplay features are used to test out gameplay ideas, and as environment artists, we use the block out phase to either build upon a level designers gray box or to form the fundamental beginnings of our own ideas for an environment.

When making environment block outs, we can quickly try out a variety of ideas generated from our initial research, references and influences. The ability to move primitive forms and proxy objects around a scene allows us to refine the composition, flow and balance of an environment before any assets are produced. With the addition of lighting and placeholder VFX, you can really begin to get a feel for your 3D world early in the development.

You can explore the world of block outs by searching for the annual hashtag #Blocktober on most popular social networks including X (formerly Twitter), Instagram and even ArtStation where games developers share their professional examples or progress on making blockouts as a challenge throughout October each year. The hashtag is certainly a great place to find ideas, inspiration and different workflow approaches to integrate into your own work.

Block outs can also be done in any 3D Digital Content Creation (DCC) package, such as Autodesk 3DS Max, Autodesk Maya, and Blender, but with Unreal Engine 5, we now have a series of tools in engine that we can use to test our ideas and get ideas out of our imagination and into the beginnings of a 3D world.

## Tools for Blocking Out in Unreal

Unreal overtime has become more multifaceted, meaning it can do more and more. In the past, artists and developers would have had to use other DCC tools such as Max and Maya to blockout/complete modeling tasks, whereas it's now quite possible to do

DOI: 10.1201/9781032663883-2

many modeling tasks within Unreal. In fact, in some stages, such as Previs, where artists create layouts, cameras and compositions, working within Unreal as much as possible is advantageous. One of the big benefits of working directly in the engine is the ability to work within the end environment. We can set up our cameras early, experiment with lighting but perhaps most importantly, press Play and walk around our block out to see how it would feel for a player and explore our ideas from all angles. Being able to model with your cameras set up gives you a good advantage over having to send files between Unreal and other DCCs.

We're going to explore a range of tools within the Modeling Mode that we can use to create block outs. The key tools to be aware of for blocking out are:

- **Parametric Primitive Creation Tools (Create)** – This set of tools includes a range of primitives and other options to create geometry directly inside your scene. The tools include the creation of parametric primitives including Box, Sphere, Cylinder and Cone meshes, as well as more complex shapes including Torus, Arrow and Stairs objects. We can also create 2D shapes including Rectangles and Discs to be used with additional tools later on including extrusions and Boolean operations. We can also draw splines and extrude and revolve paths, just like we can inside our favorite modeling package.

- **CubeGrid (Create)** – CubeGrid also allows us to create geometry directly in our environment however, unlike the parametric objects, where once you have created them, the process is complete, with cube grid you continue working after the initial creation to modify your mesh using a three-dimensional grid to push and pull faces. CubeGrid can also be used to modify existing geometry created using the parametric tools.

- **Model Tools (Model)** – Unreal's modeling tools allow us to create basic shapes quickly. There are many robust tools that allow us to build primitive buildings, natural shapes like rocks and simple organics. At present, it's not going to replace your favorite polygon modeling package or sculpting tools but it can certainly inform your blockout, previs and/or concepting phase.

While we are exploring the tools within the Modeling Mode, there are some others which may come in useful as an artist using Unreal Engine:

- **Mesh Processing (Mesh)** – Unreal also provides many tools to simplify and reduce your geometry. It's quite easy for meshes created with the modeling tools to be a bit dense in terms of topology. Fortunately, we can reduce the resolution to make things more performant. Again, like the previous two sections, we suggest you use the in-engine tools here for concepting and speedy creation for now.

- **UV Tools (UVs)** – Much like the modeling tools, Unreal provides many UV tools to help prepare meshes for texturing. Similar to the aforementioned tools, currently, these tools will not replace your traditional DCC processes but they are developing in a fast pace with new improvements coming with every version of the engine.

- **Mesh Attributes (Attribs)** – This panel of tools gives us access to a whole host of different tools which allow us to work on the mesh. Some of the common ones we use are the Edit Materials tool and the various Collision Mesh tools. The Edit Materials tool allows us to set the Material ID of each polygon, allowing us to decide which material is applied to which parts of our models. The Collision Mesh tools, as their name suggests, allow us to create and modify collision meshes, for blockouts, this can be useful to be able to test how a player may navigate around your environment.

## The Unreal Engine Viewport

Before we get started, there are a few settings in the Unreal Engine viewport that we want to make sure are set up properly to assist us when building worlds. The area we want to check is the top right set of icons and values, which show the snapping values for Translation (position), Rotation and Scale. Set these to all be turned on (the icon should be blue if enabled, if gray, the snaps are disabled. To enable them again, just click the icon) and set to *10*, *10°* and *0.5*, respectively. If your values don't match those, click the numbers next to each icon and select the appropriate value.

## Exploring the Tools

To give you a taste of these tools, we're going to explore some of them while we create a blockout for the castle in the scene we are building throughout this book. Figure 2.1 shows what the final castle looks like and while normally we would work from a piece of concept art or a series of photographs, we are using this set of isometric renders to give you a target that matches the final castle.

### Blocking Out the Main Tower

This series of instructions will guide you through creating a blockout of the castle, we are going to start by creating a new level to build our block out in. This allows us to build in isolation which is sometimes helpful when creating blockouts of hero assets such as the castle. Let's get started:

1. First, let's create the level, navigate to **File | New** or press CTRL+N.
2. From the **New Level** dialog, select **Basic Level** and click **Create**.

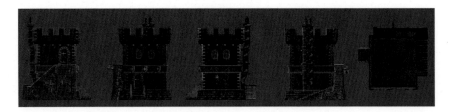

**FIGURE 2.1**    A series of isometric renders of the final castle mesh.

3. Unreal should now give you an empty level, save it by navigating to **File |
   Save Current Level As** or by pressing CTRL+S.
4. Name the level *CastleBlockOut* and save it in the **Content | Maps** folder.

With the level created, we can now start blocking out by creating a series of primitives
to layout the main shapes of the castle before refining them with the modeling tools.
We are going to work at 0,0,0 to make the creation of meshes easier, this also makes
the instructions below easier to follow:

1. Before we can create any meshes, we need to change our editor mode from
   **Selection Mode** to **Modeling Mode**, this can be done by selecting the desired
   mode from the dropdown in the top toolbar or by pressing SHIFT+5.
2. From the **Create** tools, Click the **Box** button and click anywhere in the viewport to create a 100 × 100 × 100 box mesh.
3. In the viewport overlay, set the position to *0.0, 0.0, 0.0*.
4. In the Create Box panel, set the following parameters (as shown in
   Figure 2.2):
   - **Width:** *970.0*
   - **Depth:** *1100.00*
   - **Height:** *1450.0*
5. Click the **Accept** Button in the viewport overlay.

We now need to create three more boxes, one for the base of the castle, one for the red
section around the middle of the castle and one for the top section.

1. Create the box for the base of the castle at *0.0, 0.0, 0.0* and set the param-
   eters to:
   - **Width:** *1200*
   - **Depth:** *1300*
   - **Height:** *250*
2. Create the box for the red section at *0.0, 0.0, 680.0* and set the parameters to:

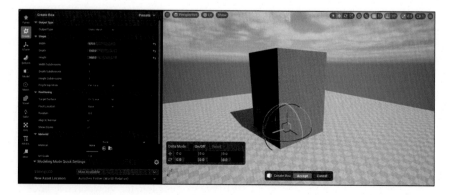

**FIGURE 2.2**   The first box of the block out in creation mode.

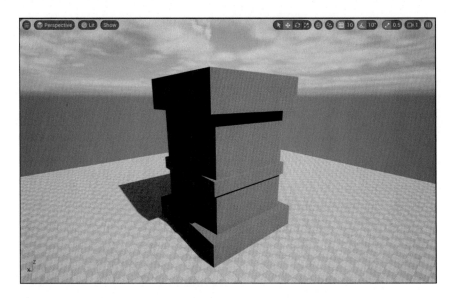

**FIGURE 2.3**    The basic castle forms, made from the four boxes.

- **Width:** *1050*
- **Depth:** *1150*
- **Height:** *150*

3. Create the box for the top of the castle at *0.0, 0.0, 1450.0* and set the parameters to:

- **Width:** *1200*
- **Depth:** *1300*
- **Height:** *360*

You should now have four blocks forming the very basic shape of our castle, similar to that shown in Figure 2.3.

With the main forms in place, we can now add some refinements to better match our target image. If you refer back to Figure 2.1, you will notice that the base section is tapered to be wider at the bottom and the top section, as well as having battlements (which we will look at later), also has a tapered lower section to make a more interesting silhouette. Let's look at modifying our simple blocks to match those forms, starting with the base:

1. Select the box that forms the lower section of the castle in the viewport.
2. In the **Model** section of the Modeling Mode tools, select the **PolyGroup Edit** tool, this will allow us to modify the polygons which form the mesh.
3. Select the top face, this should cause a transform gizmo to appear, as shown in Figure 2.4.
4. You can now either modify the scale of the face using the sections of the gizmo which look like square braces [ ] or by typing into the viewport overlay.

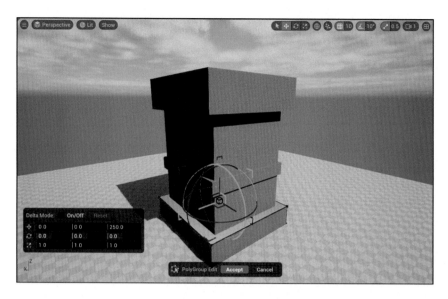

**FIGURE 2.4** The transform gizmo in the viewport when editing a polygon in polygroup edit.

- If using the overlay, type 0.9 into both the X (red) and Y (green) scale values. You will see them immediately swap back to 1.0, this is normal.
5. Once you are happy with the shape, click the **Accept** button.

Now we can move onto the top block:

1. Select the top block and again, select the **PolyGroup Edit** tool.
2. Select the bottom face and then click the **Bevel** button.
3. Set the **Bevel Distance** to *50.0*.
4. Click the **Apply** button to return to the **PolyGroup Edit** tool menu.
5. Click the **Accept** button in the viewport.

Before we move onto the battlements on the top of the castle, let's refine the shape of the middle section to better match the silhouette shown in the reference, to do this, we are going to need to add some more geometry to the model, we can do this using the Insert Edge Loop tool.

1. Select the middle block and once again open the **PolyGroup Edit** tool.
2. Click the **Insert Edge Loop** button.
3. Set the following parameters:
   - **Position Mode:** Even
   - **Insertion Mode:** Plane Cut
   - **Num Loops:** 2
4. Click on one of the vertical edges, this should add two edges into the mesh, as shown on the left in Figure 2.5.

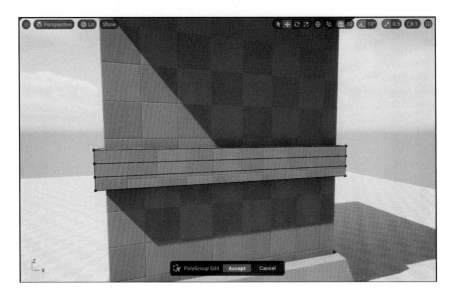

**FIGURE 2.5**   Insert edge loop tool with two even, plane cut loops added to the middle section.

5. Click the **Done** button in the **PolyGroup Edit** panel.
6. Whilst holding down SHIFT, click each of the middle polygons from each side of the block.
7. Click the **Push Pull** button and move your mouse to inset the selected faces, clicking in the viewport when you are happy with the adjustment.
8. Click the **Accept** button.

The primary form silhouette of the castle should now be taking shape. You should have something that looks similar to the castle in Figure 2.6.

## Adding the Embattlements with CubeGrid

Next, we are going to refine the top of the castle to add the embattlements (or crenellations). We are going to make use of one of Unreal Engine 5's newer block out tools, CubeGrid. CubeGrid allows us to create and modify meshes using a 3D grid which we can rotate and scale to our needs. We're going to use it for a relatively simple solution but the tool really excels when being used for blocking out levels.

1. Select the top block of the castle.
2. From the **Create** tools, select **CubeGrid**.
3. Click the **Reset Grid from Actor** button, this will snap the grid to align with the bottom of the block.
4. Set the following parameter in the CubeGrid Tool dialog:
   - **Grid Frame Origin:** *0.0, 0.0, 1810.0* – This will align the grid to the top of the block.
   - **Current Block Size:** *50.0.*

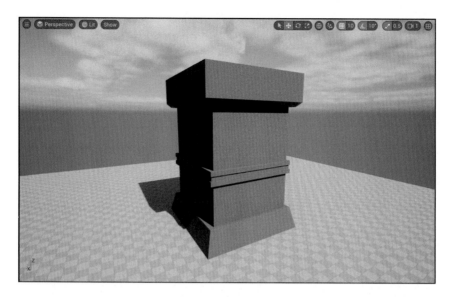

**FIGURE 2.6** The castle so far with primitive forms and minor changes.

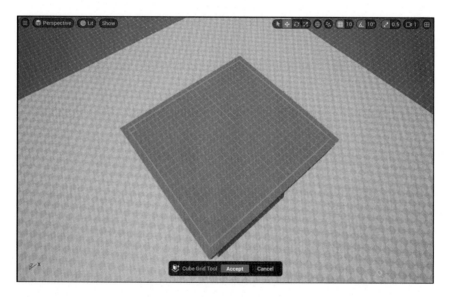

**FIGURE 2.7** CubeGrid selection for the top of the castle.

5. Drag on the grid to select all of the grid squares inside the block, leaving a 1 square outline, as shown in Figure 2.7.
6. Click the **Push** button, three times (you can press Q instead if you prefer).
7. To make the embattlements, select grid squares and lower them using push, 1 square. If you make a mistake, you can either undo (Ctrl+Z) or use Pull (E key) to bring the block back up.

**FIGURE 2.8**   The completed embattlements using CubeGrid.

The castle isn't square so the pattern for each side will need to be different to get something that looks pleasing, remember, this is just a block out, so we are aiming to present an idea, not build a final, polished asset. The patterns we used (see Figure 2.8) include three blocks in each corner remaining untouched and then:

- For the shorter side, a pattern of pushing two squares down and leaving two squares up which we will refer to using notation of 2D, 2U for simplicity.
- For the longer side, the pattern was as follows: 2D, 2U, 2D, 3U, 2D, 3U, 2D, 2U, 2D.

When you have finished, remember to close the tool by clicking the **Accept** button.

## Adding Stairs to the Block Out

Next we are going to add two sets of stairs, one set for the front door and one set which runs around the building to the second floor. We are going to make them using Unreal's built-in stairs tool and boxes for the landing sections between each set of stairs and sides of the front stairs.

### *Front Stairs*

Let's start with the front stairs.

1. From the **Create** tools, select the **Stairs** tool.
2. Click in the viewport to place the stairs in the world.
3. In the viewport overlay, set the position of the stairs to *–750.0, –250.0, 0.0,* ensuring that Delta Mode is not checked.
4. Set the following parameters in the Create Stairs dialog:

- **Number of Steps:** *13*
- **Step Width:** *300.0*
- **Step Height:** *18.0*
- **Step Depth:** *24.0*

5. Click the **Accept** button.

With the stair object in place, next we can create the sides of the stairs, we are going to do this using the PolyGroup Edit tools once more.

1. Create a new Box in the viewport, position it at *–750.0, –80.0, 0.0* and set the following parameters:
   - **Width:** *50.0*
   - **Depth:** *400.0*
   - **Height:** *350.0*
2. Click **Accept** and then with the new box selected, and open the **PolyGroup Edit** tool from the **Model** tools section.
3. Use the **Insert Edge Loop** tool to add a vertical edge in line with the edge of the top step of the stairs object. Set **Position Mode** to *Proportion Offset* to be able to select where the loop goes by clicking on an edge to be dissected, where you want the loop to be. When you have added the edge, click the **Done** button in the **PolyGroup Edit** panel.
4. Select the top, front edge of the box, using the gizmo, lower it until the angle of the top face matches the angle of the stairs. Alternatively, you can set the Z (blue) variable in the viewport overlay to *90.0*.
5. Click the **Accept** button. The stairs should now look like the example in Figure 2.9.

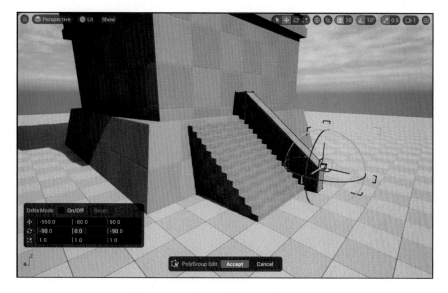

**FIGURE 2.9**  The stairs with the side structure added.

6. To create the other side of the stairs, hold ALT on the keyboard and drag the object in the Y-axis, this should duplicate it. The other side of the stairs needs to be placed at *–750.0, –420.0, 0.0* which you can set in the **Details** panel if you don't want to align it by eye in the viewport.

With the front steps in place, we can move on to the stairs that wrap around the back and left side of the building.

### Wrap Around Stairs

We will once again be using the stair tool again but before we do, let's put some boxes in so we know where the stairs need to go.

1. Using the **Box** tool from the **Create** menu, add a new box to the world, position it at *–300.0, –630.0, 0.0* and the set the parameters as follows:
   - **Width:** *300.0*
   - **Depth:** *500.0*
   - **Height:** *865.0*
2. Click the **Accept** button.
3. Repeat the process for a second box, positioning it at *370.0, –630.0, 0.0*. Set the following parameters:
   - **Width:** *300.0*
   - **Depth:** *850.0*
   - **Height:** *360.0*
4. Click the **Accept** button.

With the boxes in place, we can now add the stair objects, we are going to create two new stair objects with different parameters:

1. Using the **Stairs** tool from the **Create** menu, add a set of stairs. Set the position to *670.0, –30.0, 0.0* and the rotation to *0.0, 0.0, –90.0*.
2. Set the following parameters:
   - **Number of Steps:** *15*
   - **Step Width:** *250.0*
   - **Step Height:** *23.0*
   - **Step Depth:** *60.0*
3. Click the **Accept** button.
4. Add a second set of stairs at the position *250.0, –630.0, 360.0* with a rotation of *0.0, 0.0, 180.0* and the following parameters:
   - **Number of Steps:** *15*
   - **Step Width:** *300.0*

- **Step Height:** *32.0*
- **Step Depth:** *40.0*

5. Click the **Accept** button

With the stairs added to the block out, the last element of the major forms to add is the chimney at the back of the castle.

## Adding the Chimney

To add the chimney, we are going to begin with a box and use the modeling tools to make the wiggly form you can see in Figure 2.1 from earlier in the chapter.

1. From the **Create** menu, add a **Box** at location *550.0, 70.0, 250.0.*
2. Set the parameters of the box to:
   - **Width:** *200.0*
   - **Depth:** *100.0*
   - **Height:** *200.0*
3. Click the **Accept** button.

We are now going to use the PolyGroup Edit tools to make the shape of the chimney. For this, we are going to use the **Extrude** tool and then the transform gizmo in the viewport to rotate and move selected faces to get the desired shape. We are going to leave you to do this one by eye after the first extrusion:

1. Select the new box and from the **Model** menu, select the **PolyGroup Edit** tool.
2. Click the top face of the box and press the **Extrude** button.
3. Move your mouse in the viewport, you should see the extrusion following your mouse (assuming the tools **Distance Mode** is still set to **Click in Viewport**), position your mouse so there is a small extrusion and click in the viewport.
4. Using the viewport gizmo, rotate the face away from the castle and, if required, move the face back toward the castle to create a corner.
5. Repeat the extrusions, rotations and moves, to make the shape for the chimney, feel free to play around here if you want to.

The main forms of the castle are now blocked in, you should have something that resembles the block out shown in Figure 2.10.

We could, if we wanted, add a few more simple shapes to help show some forms, such as boxes for the chimney braces, cylinders for chimney pots on top of the chimney, and a thin block for the side on the side of the stairs.

**FIGURE 2.10**   The "completed" blockout of the castle with a chimney.

## Reusing a Block Out

When we block out things like the castle in a separate map, we will want to place the result in our world with landscapes or even reuse them in multiple places. There are a couple of different approaches we can take to make that possible, we are going to explore two great options.

### Packed Level Actors

The first of these approaches is to create a Packed Level Actor. This creates us an empty level with any actors we choose (meshes, lights, blueprints etc.) which can be used as a sublevel (which we explore later) and also a placeable Blueprint actor. To create a packed-level actor:

1. Select all of the meshes we have created to make the castle block out. Do not select the floor or any of the other actors in the world.
2. Right Click with the mouse over the selected meshes and select **Level | Create Packed Level Actor...**
3. From the pop-up check that External Actors is checked and that the **Pivot Type** is set to *Centre Min Z*.
4. In the **Save Level As** dialog box, navigate to **Content | Maps** and create a new folder with CTRL+SHIFT+N, call it *PackedLevelActors*. Name the new Map *CastleBlockOut* and click **Save**.
5. A second dialog, **Save Asset As** will now appear. Keep the Path and Name the same, simply click the **Save** button.

You should now have two new assets, a map and a blueprint:

- If you drag the Blueprint into the current level, you will see a single blueprint actor which contains all of the meshes, but can be moved as a single asset.
- If you open the map (and set the view mode to Unlit), you will see the meshes we created, as separate actors.

## Merged Actor

The second approach is to merge the meshes into a single static mesh actor. This approach can only be used when we are creating a collection of meshes, you cannot merge lights etc. using this approach.

1. If you followed the previous steps, you won't be able to do this in your existing level, instead, you will need to open the **CastleBlockOut** level from **Content | Maps** and swap the view mode to Unlit in order to be able to see the meshes.
2. Select all of the meshes we have created to make the castle block out.
3. From the top menu navigate to **Actor | Merge Actors | Merge**.
4. This will open the **Create Merged Actor** dialog, navigate to **Content | Meshes** and set the **Name** to *CastleBlockOut_Mesh*.
5. If you double click the **CastleBlockOut_Mesh** asset that this process creates, you will see your castle model in the Static Mesh Editor, this can be used in a level in the same way any imported static mesh from a DCC can.

## Conclusion

With the block out now reusable, we've come to the end of the chapter. In this chapter, we've discussed the reasons why we block out and explored the modeling tools to create a block out of our castle. In Chapter 3, we will be exploring landscapes and learning about how we block out landscapes using the landscape tool. Before we move on, let's check what you've learned with a quick quiz.

## Chapter 2 Quiz

Question 1: What is the main purpose of a block out?
   a. To procrastinate at the start of a project.
   b. To build meshes in engine instead of a DCC, making environment artists obsolete.
   c. To test ideas and begin to answer questions about the world.
   d. To make objects with a fun gray grid pattern on them.

Question 2: How do we duplicate a model in the viewport?

    a. CTRL+D.

    b. CTRL+C, CTRL+V.

    c. ALT Click Drag.

    d. All of the above.

Question 3: Which tool allows us to make polygon editing operations?

    a. Edit Poly.

    b. PolyGroup Edit.

    c. CubeGrid.

    d. All of the above.

Question 4: Which Position Mode in the Insert Edge Loop loop (part of the PolyGroup Edit tools) allows us to insert a number of edges an equal distance apart?

    a. Even.

    b. Proportion Offset.

    c. Distance Offset.

    d. None of the above.

## Answers

Question 1: c

Question 2: d

Question 3: b

Question 4: a

# 3

## Introduction to Unreal Landscapes

### Introduction to Landscapes

Creating Landscapes for games can require a lot of DCC tools to pull together high-quality assets. We have provided several starting assets that will help you along this process including a Heightmap and several texture sets. In addition to what we've provided you may wish to supplement your learning by exploring landscape creation in packages such as a Houdini, Gaea and World Machine along with texture generation using Megascans and Substance Designer. These additional tools are not required to complete any of the exercises in this book, they are simply suggestions for you to explore in your own time to discover additional development opportunities.

In Unreal, we have access to a wide variety of dedicated tools to help create massive worlds for games and real time applications. We'll begin our journey into this toolset by exploring the sculpting and initial setup tools. In this chapter, we'll get started by Learning about the Landscape Mode and how we can utilize it to begin our own Landscape.

### Common Approaches to Landscape Creation

Before we use the tools, it is worth exploring common approaches to creating Landscapes in Unreal. The most common approaches are:

1. Create a new Landscape within the editor using Unreals Landscape Sculpting Tools.
2. Import a Landscape Heightmap Texture that generates our Landscape automatically.
3. Build a custom Landscape plugin that imports Landscape data from external programs.
4. Import simple 3D meshes, for smaller worlds and environments where exterior terrain is limited to say a small garden or courtyard.

In this chapter, we are going to focus on the first two options from the aforementioned list. We'll explore the first option now to explore how we can create Landscapes from scratch.

DOI: 10.1201/9781032663883-3

## Starting a New Landscape

When beginning a Landscape, it's helpful to review Epic's Landscape Technical Guide. Epic's guide demonstrates how landscapes are broken down into components and sections that create an overall resolution and total components number. Each component contains height data stored in a texture. Components are divided up into either 1 or 4 sections to increase the resolution of the overall landscape. The components also contain quads and vertices which represent the geometry. To help limit what's drawn at any one time, the landscape sections are limited to specific amounts of quads, which we can select from a drop-down menu.

The terminology used is designed to help the game engine break up large landscapes to ensure they render effectively. For your first landscape, it may be a little overwhelming, but it will become second nature very quickly.

Let's begin! In the following exercise, we are assuming you've already built the level from Chapter 1. You can of course try these techniques on a project of your own if you prefer.

1. Click on the **File Menu**, select **Open Level**.
2. Locate your **WizardsDesk_Main** level in **Content | Maps | WizardsDesk | levels** and Double Click on it to load it.
3. Open up the **Levels** panel, double click on **WizardsDesk_Landscape** to make it the current level. This will ensure our created landscape is placed in this sub level.
4. Change the editor mode to **Landscape Mode** by clicking **Selection Mode** and using the drop-down menu to select **Landscape** or by pressing Shift+2.
5. If you have no existing landscapes in your level, you will be presented with the **Manage** tab. The **Manage** tab allows us to Create a New Landscape from scratch or create one by Importing a Height Map from File.

You'll now see a lot of controls, let's explore a few of the concepts before creating our first Landscape. Epic recommends a Maximum of 1024 Total Components, this value is near the bottom of the options menu. Increasing the Overall Resolution slider will automatically increase the Number of Components and Total Components. This gives us an easy way to track the cost of our Landscape. But what numbers should we use and why?

Well, it's a balancing act, we want to be able to render our world with both an efficient resolution and components numbers. If we go too low, the landscape will look bad and level of detail changes may be very visible, however if we go too high, the game may experience CPU bottlenecks as it tries to deal with too many draw calls.

We have included a couple of example Landscape Sizes (Table 3.1), which represent frequently used landscapes in Unreal, this can be seen in Figure 3.1, you can also view a larger table on Epic's website.

It's helpful to consider landscape size in meters versus resolution. For example, 1009×1009 vertices could represent roughly a 1 km×1 km Landscape. However, if you create a Landscape in another DCC you may need to do some conversion Math.

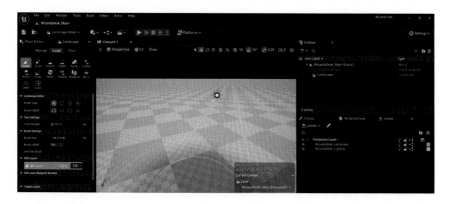

**FIGURE 3.1** Landscape creation.

**TABLE 3.1**

Landscape Setup Details

| Overall Resolution | Section Size | Sections Per Component | Number of Components | Total Components |
| --- | --- | --- | --- | --- |
| 8129 × 8129 | 127 | 4 (2 × 2) | 32 × 32 | 1024 |
| 4033 × 4033 | 63 | 4 (2 × 2) | 32 × 32 | 1024 |
| 2017 × 2017 | 63 | 4 (2 × 2) | 16 × 16 | 256 |
| 1009 × 1009 | 63 | 4 (2 × 2) | 8 × 8 | 64 |
| 1009 × 1009 | 63 | 1 (1 × 1) | 16 × 16 | 256 |

For example, if you create a 5-km Landscape in another package using a resolution of 1009 vertices your X and Y scale in Unreal would be $100\times5000/1009$. If you are ever unsure you can always use your middle mouse button in Unreals top viewport to draw a measuring line along your landscape's axis to reveal its size in Unreal (note this will be in centimeters).

As with most things in games development, rules are there to be broken, it is quite possible to create landscapes with no relation to real-world units or concern in regards to performance. While working on a small portfolio piece, you may find some creative freedom liberating, but note that building landscapes with real-world values will keep your level of detail and consistency in line with others.

## Working with Landscape Mode

Now that we've covered some technical theory let's build our first Landscape.

1. Click on the **File Menu**, select **Open Level**.
2. Locate the **WizardsDesk_Main** level in **Content | Maps | WizardsDesk | levels** and Double Click to load it.

3. Open up the **Levels** panel, double click on **WizardsDesk_Landscape** to make it the current level. This will ensure our created landscape is placed in this **Sub Level**.

4. Change the editor mode to **Landscape Mode** by clicking **Selection Mode** and using the drop down menu to select **Landscape** or by pressing SHIFT+2.

5. Using the **Manage** tab, set the **Section Size** to *63×63*, **Section Per Component** to *1*, **Number of Components** to *16* to achieve an **Overall Resolution** of *1009*.

6. Click **Create**.

7. If you change the Viewport Viewmode to **Unlit** you will now see the created Landscape Actor with a default gray checker material applied. To do this click the **Lit** button in the top left of the viewport and select **Unlit** or use ALT+3.

8. Change the editor mode back to **Selection** by clicking **Landscape Mode** and using the drop-down menu to select **Selection** or by pressing SHIFT+1.

9. To view the level in **Lit** mode you will need to add a Directional Light to the level. To do this Navigate to the **Place Actor** panel (if yours is not open you can access it via the **Window** Menu). Click on the Light Bulb icon, then drag and drop a **Directional Light** anywhere into the level. You can then change the Viewport Viewmode back to **Lit**. Doing this helps us preview the Landscape as we make changes to its shape.

10. Lastly, change the mode back to **Landscape Mode** by clicking the **Selection Mode** and using the drop-down menu or by pressing SHIFT+2. Your world should now match the image shown in Figure 3.1. We are now ready to explore the sculpting tools.

## Using Landscape Sculpting Tools

If you have followed on from the previous activity you will see an active white ring cursor and a shadow projected on the Landscape. If this is the case, you will now be able to sculpt and interact with the Landscape. If, however, you changed the mode or are reading this section later, you will need to go back to Landscape Mode and change the Landscape tab to Sculpt. Make sure to do this and let's now review the Sculpt Brush options.

The Sculpt Brush has three actions, these are:

1. To add height to the landscape, Left Clicking on the landscape with the Sculpt Brush active will carry out this action.

2. To lower the landscape, use the Sculpt Brush with the following controls CTRL+SHIFT+Left Click.

3. To smooth the landscape, use the Sculpt Brush with the following controls SHIFT+Left Click.

In addition to these basic actions, you can also increase or decrease the Sculpt Brush size with the square bracket keys [ and ].

**FIGURE 3.2** Landscape sculpt brush settings.

Figure 3.2 shows the overall UI options for our brushes. Let's review these:

1. **Brush Type** – This controls how the brush interacts with the landscape, for example, a smooth round brush, added texture/s and or brush across an entire component.
2. **Brush Falloff** – This controls the fading of the stroke on the landscape.
3. **Tool Strength** – This value controls the amount of distance the Landscape is deformed during sculpting. For finesse sculpting, you may find values as low as 0.1–0.3 helpful, whereas higher values are good for shape layout and blocking out the landscape.
4. **Brush Size** – This is the overall radius of the brush.
5. **Brush Falloff** – This determines the percentage of the brush that should feature falloff.

6. **Clay Brush** – This creates a more additive approach to sculpting. You might find this preferable if you enjoy digital sculpting in other DCC's such as ZBrush or Blender.

Using only the Sculpt Brush, adjust the Landscape to roughly match Figure 3.3. Work on big shapes first, building up the background hills, then dig in a plateau in the center of the landscape before finishing with a river channel. Try not to spend too long on this activity, the goal is to blockout large shapes swiftly to test out ideas.

---

**USEFUL TIP**

The Tool Strength for Brushes can go above one. Don't assume that the tool options have maximums and minimums because it looks that way on the UI. It's great to go above the maximum values when sculpting very large terrains.

---

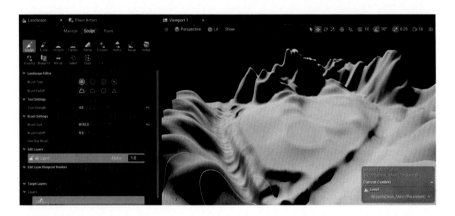

**FIGURE 3.3**   Landscape sculpt target 1.

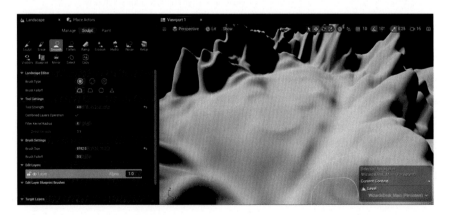

**FIGURE 3.4**   Landscape smooth brush.

The Smooth Brush can be useful if the Sculpt Brush marks are too severe or noticeable. In Figure 3.4, the area south of the plateau has been smoothed using the Smooth Brush and Left Click. The use of this tool is quite subjective however, you will most likely need a high Tool Strength when working on a large Landscape and a low one for smaller areas.

Use the Smooth brush to reduce any noticeable Brush marks in your Landscape and try to blend the overall shapes subtly together.

The Erosion Brushes are great for adding some finer detail, they work by removing volume and placing it elsewhere. There are two options, the Erosion Brush and the Hydro Erosion Brush. You'll find that the Erosion Brush will help create flat planes and sharp angles, whereas the Hydro Erosion Brush will dig into crevices and carry out rain water erosion. Both brushes have a lot of properties for you to tweak and experiment with. The erosion ability of both brushes work on the same principle that more iterations equals more erosion at the cost of viewport performance.

In addition to the Erosion Brushes, you may find the Noise Brush helpful to break up repeating patterns and brush marks. The Noise Brush offers you the ability to tweak its Noise Scale and alter the Noise Mode to adjust how it affects landscapes. It is very noticeable, so be careful not to overuse the Noise Brush and where possible combine textures with the Sculpt Brush.

**USEFUL TIP**

Try using the Noise Brush or a Sculpt Brush with a Pattern Prior to Erosion, this will help you create more detailed shapes. Eroding very soft mountains/hills can lead to quite bland shapes.

Figure 3.5 shows a basic Erosion pass using the three Brushes (Erosion, Hydro Erosion and Noise). Try to break up your mountains into more distinct shapes and best match the image shown.

Figure 3.6 demonstrates a tiny bit more visual noise to the Landscape and is the target to aim for in your own work for this chapter. If you wish to take this further you

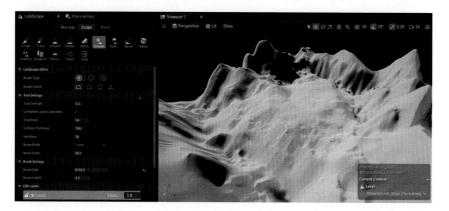

**FIGURE 3.5** Landscape erosion and noise brushes.

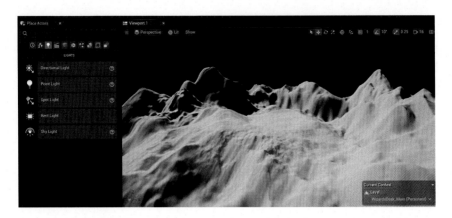

**FIGURE 3.6**   Landscape sculpt target 2.

could gather Heightmap textures to use for the sculpting brushes to push the landscape to appear more natural.

Next, we are going to explore Heightmap generation as an alternative means of creating/blocking out Landscapes. The sculpting tools in Unreal are fantastic for quick and bold shape creation but require a lot of practice to create realistic and detailed-looking scenery. In contrast, we can also import real-world Heightmap data or Heightmap generated textures from other DCC's to help create the look of our Landscape actor.

## Using Landscape Heightmaps

We are now going to explore how we can utilize Heightmaps from external DCC's to help create our Landscape Actor in Unreal. Let's get started!

1. Click on the **File Menu**, select **Open Level**.
2. Locate the **WizardsDesk_Main** level in **Content | Maps | WizardsDesk | levels** and Double Click to load it.
3. Open up the **Levels** panel, double click on **WizardsDesk_Landscape** to make it the current level. This will ensure our created landscape is placed in this **Sub Level**.
4. Change to **Landscape Mode** by clicking **Selection Mode** and using the drop-down menu or by pressing Shift + 2.
5. Open the **Manage** tab and click the **New** button.
6. Select the **Import from File** button.
7. Click on the three dots next to **Heightmap File** to open up the **File Browser**.
8. Open the provided file in the following directory **WizardDesk | Content | Landscape | LandscapeHeightmap.png**.
9. When loaded, Unreal will automatically populate the Landscape settings based on the texture resolution. You can tweak these if you wish for further resolution.

10. We now need to see the Scale, in this instance, we are going to focus on the Z. The formula we are going to use is 100×**DCCHeight/Overall Resolution**. During creation, the DCCHeight was 2500 meters and the **Image Resolution** is *1009* so the Formula is 100×2500/1009. Which gives us a Z scale of 247.770069.

11. Now click **Import.** You may review your settings against those found in Figure 3.7.

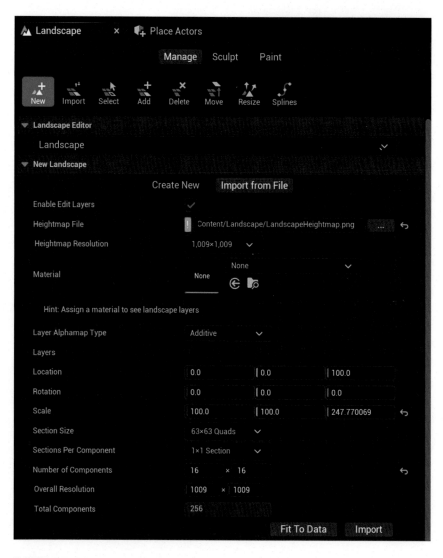

**FIGURE 3.7**   Landscape heightmap setup.

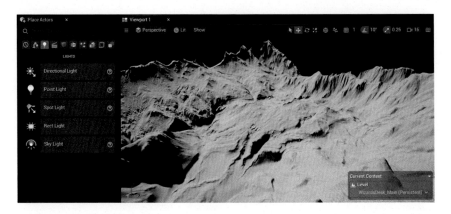

**FIGURE 3.8**   Landscape heightmap result.

12. You may find that the new landscape is under/overlapping with your previous Landscape. Use the **World Outliner** to toggle the Landscape Actors visibility and or move them using **Selection Modes** Transform tools.
13. If you are happy with the results Save your levels.

When evaluating the result in Figure 3.8, it's clear that there's a lot more subtle and natural details to the Landscape. The Heightmap makes it look extremely easy as the landscape appears out of nothing, this however, masks a lot of work completed in external DCCs/photo reference of real-world locations. This type of result is possible through manual sculpting however you will need a large library of brushes to replicate things such as accurate erosion, weathering, river channels, and so on. We will continue this adventure when we look into the Landmass Brushes later in the book as we explore a nondestructive approach.

## Conclusion

In this chapter, we've reviewed many of the required elements to create our first Landscape Actor. We've gone through a basic sculpting workflow and compared the provided tools to a Heightmap generated Landscape. On the surface, it may appear that the Heightmap approach from external tools is ideal, however, we always want to do exploratory work in Unreal first that then informs more detailed landscape generation. The rough sculpting approach mentioned in this chapter can be refined and still used for the final artifact, however, you will need to build up a library of Landscape Height Maps to achieve a similar level of detail.

In Chapter 4, we'll begin to explore simple Landscape Materials to help render our worlds. But before we do, let's review this chapter's quiz.

## Chapter 3  Quiz

Question 1: What is the Landscape Mode used for in Unreal Engine?

a. Landscape Mode enables us to set up, sculpt and paint Landscape Actors within Unreal Engine.

b. Landscape Mode enables us to paint foliage within Unreal Engine.

c. Landscape Mode allows us to place land in Unreal Engine.

Question 2: What is a Landscape Actor?

a. A Landscape Actor controls the position of our Landscapes in Unreal Editor. It also has options for Materials and RVT texture generation.

b. A Landscape Actor connects other Actors such as Lights and Sound VFX to our Landscape system.

c. Landscape Actors is a special Actor that has special properties which allow it to be sculpted, painted and customized for World Building.

Question 3: What are Heightmaps?

a. Height maps are maps that are found on the top of high areas in a level.

b. Height maps are grayscale textures that control how rough a pixel is (White being Rough and Black being smooth).

c. Height maps are grayscale textures that are used to displace a vertex position (White being high and Black being low).

Question 4: What is one of the problems with Unreal's Landscape Sculpting Tools?

a. The default Landscape Authoring tools are quite soft and round. It's helpful to import brush textures and or use erosion tools to break up the soft shapes.

b. The default Landscape Authoring tools are destructive, each action removes history of the previous action which makes it difficult to make subtle changes.

c. The default Landscape Authoring tools lack complex layer modes to track blending of user actions.

d. All of the above.

## Answers

Question 1: a

Question 2: c

Question 3: c

Question 4: d

# 4

## Introduction to Unreal Landscape Materials

### Introduction to Landscape Materials

This chapter introduces you to the Material Creation for your Landscapes, you'll learn about:

- What we use Landscape Materials for.
- How to construct your own Landscape Material.
- How to begin painting Landscape Materials in Unreal.

Landscape Materials are bespoke Materials that are applied to our Landscapes inside Unreal Levels. They have specific functionality that control the blending and application of textures to Unreal Landscape Actors. Landscape Material functionality is tailored depending on the scope and type of terrain, however some features such as Texture Tiling, Blending, Slope Control and Mesh Instancing are very common across most materials.

In this chapter, we'll begin by looking at some of the more common Landscape Material requirements before applying these in a final material.

### Landscape Material Requirements

Before we begin creating our Landscape Material, let's look at the common ingredients and assets that an artist might use.

- **Textures** – As per most Materials, textures form the backbone of the required assets. For Landscape Materials, there are two main types of textures:
  - **Surface Textures** – This includes things like Colour, Normal and Roughness textures for Landscape areas such as grass.
  - **Utility Textures** – This includes things like Masks, MixMaps and other kinds of blending textures that help control how Surface Textures are drawn.
- **Tiling Controls** – Tiling Controls afford us the ability to repeat a texture, or a series of textures over a surface. Landscape Materials require this feature as they are enormous and present us with a unique challenge as we can often see landscapes up close and in the distance. This creates the need for a distance-based tiling. In addition to distance concerns, we might also want to vary the way

DOI: 10.1201/9781032663883-4

our textures are tiled to help break up repetition or texture seams. There are a variety of ways of achieving this such as noise blends, gradient maps and Texture Bombing, however, these processes can become quite expensive at runtime.

- **Slope Control** – We may wish for specific textures or surfaces to render on certain slopes. For example, we may not want grass or trees to appear on an almost vertical slope. Having the ability to read in the angle or adjust blending due to the normal of a surface is an excellent way to control texturing.
- **Height Control** – Height Control can be viewed in a couple of different ways, we can blend different textures based on the overall Z height of a landscape. Alternatively, we can use Heightmap textures and functions to help blend Landscape Textures using grayscale Heightmaps. The former is often used for introducing weather changes, such as a snow layer at a specific Z altitude.
- **Layer Blending** – Landscape Materials are commonly broken down into layers, the layers represent different types of materials such as Grass, Rock, Stone and or Snow. We can Blend Landscape Layers in three ways: Weight, Alpha and Height.
  - Weight is best when you want to import textures from DCCs to control blending, you are able to manipulate the blend in any order.
  - Alpha is great when you want a precise layer order such that removing a layer might reveal something underneath.
  - Height works in the same way as weight but allows you to improve the blend between different layers with a Heightmap texture giving you more control.
- **Runtime Virtual Texturing** – This is a common technology where texel Data are provided to the GPU at runtime. Runtime Virtual Texturing (RVT) is commonly used for landscapes as it helps in caching complex Landscape Materials resulting in performance improvements. RVT also affords Subtle Blending of non-landscape actors with the Landscape Materials. A common use of this could be at the base of rocks or trees. This helps create the illusion of meshes being part of the world and avoid obvious joins and intersections.

These technologies are just some of the features that might be present in Landscape Materials. We will explore some more in later chapters. One thing to remember is just because we can add something doesn't mean we should, there's always a balance between artistic needs and performance. It'll be up to you to decide what's most important for your worlds and Landscape Materials.

## Creating Our First Landscape Material

Let's now build our first Landscape Material. We will start simple and add to our Landscape Material overtime.

1. Click on the **File** menu, and select **Open Level**.
2. You can choose to load the **Landscape_Material_Start** level found in **Content | Maps** or if you are following on from a previous chapter, feel free

to use the **WizardsDesk_Main** level in **Content | Maps | WizardsDesk | levels** and Double Click to load it.

- The **Landscape_Material_Start** Level has the added Buildings and a bit more decoration for fun.

3. Open up the **Levels** panel, double click on **WizardsDesk_Landscape** to make it the current level. This will ensure our created Landscape is placed in this **Sub Level**.

4. Using the **Content Browser** navigate to **Content | Materials**, if there is not a Materials folder create one by Right Clicking in the **Content** folder and selecting **New Folder**, label the new folder *Materials*.

5. Next, check to see if there is a **Master** sub folder inside of the **Materials** Folder. If there isn't one, Right Click in the **Materials** folder and select **New Folder** and label the folder *Master*.

6. Once inside the **Master** folder, Right Click and select **New Material**. Label the Material *M_Landscape*.

7. Double Click on our new **M_Landscape** material. Right Click in the **Material Graph** and from the menu search for *Landscape Layer Blend*.

8. Select the **Landscape Layer Blend** node and add three **Layers** to the array using the + button in the **Details** panel. Set the **Layer Name property** to **[0]**=*Mud,* **[1]**=*Grass,* and **[2]**=*Stone.*

9. Set the **Blend Type** to **LB_Weight_Blend** for each array entry and lastly set the **Preview Weight** to *1* on array entry **[0]**. This makes at least one of the layers fully active by default.

10. Navigate to the folder **Content | Textures | Landscape** folder in the **Content Browser**. Select the following textures; **Landscape_Grass_BaseColor, Landscape_Mud_BaseColor,** and **Landscape_Stone_BaseColor.**

11. Drag and drop the selected textures into the **M_Landscape** material graph.

12. Connect the **Texture Samples** to the corresponding inputs on the **Landscape Layer Blend Node**.
    - **Landscape_Mud_BaseColour** connects to the **Mud** layer.
    - **Landscape_Grass_BaseColor** connects to the **Grass** layer.
    - **Landscape_Stone_BaseColor** connects to the **Stone** layer.

13. Connect the output of the **Landscape Layer Blend Node** to the **Base Color** input of the material output node.

14. Save your Material, review Figure 4.1 to ensure your material is the same.

Next, we will preview the Material so far on our Landscape. To do this, we are going to use the Landscape Actor in the World Outliner. For the next section, we will be using the Landscape generated from the Heightmap discussed in Chapter 3. If you do not have a Landscape Actor ready to Texture, you can open the provided **Landscape_Material_Start** level which you can find in **Content | Maps**.

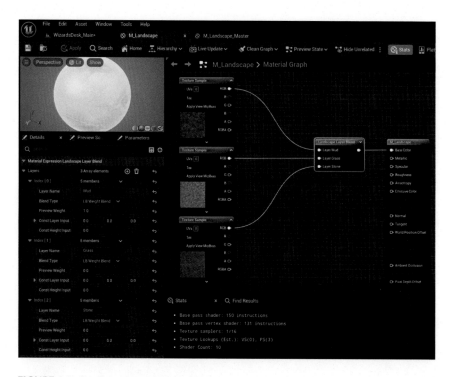

**FIGURE 4.1**   Landscape material layer blend.

## Applying and Painting Our First Landscape Material

With a Landscape Actor ready, we can move on!

1. With your **Landscape** actor selected use the **Detail** panel to find the **Landscape Material** property. Set the **Landscape Material** property to use our material **M_Landscape**.

2. To preview our **Landscape Material**, we need to set up some options in **Landscape Mode**. Switch to **Landscape Mode** and swap over to the **Paint** tab.

3. Scroll to the bottom of the **Paint** tab and you should see our Landscape Material's **Layers** listed. See Figure 4.2 for an example.

4. These **Layers** are created when you apply a **Material** to a **Landscape** that utilizes the **Material Landscape Layer Blend** node in the Material Graph. When the **Layer Info** is created, they are set to **None**, you need to click on the + button next to each layer to setup and save a Layer Info asset. Figure 4.3 shows an example of what the + button does. Ideally, you want to save **Layer Info** together in a sensible location that is relevant to the Level/Landscape.

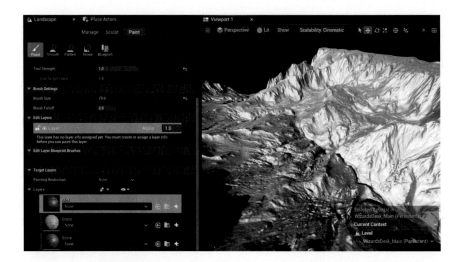

**FIGURE 4.2**    Landscape material layer info.

**FIGURE 4.3**    Saving material layer info.

5. Once this is done you can now paint on the **Landscape Layers**. To do this, it's a matter of selecting the **Layers** in the **Paint** tab and then painting on the Landscape Actor using the Left Mouse Button. Much like the **Sculpt** tab, the **Paint** tab has similar functionality to set the **Brush Size** and **Tool Strength**.

6. Try experimenting and painting on the Landscape at this point, Figure 4.4 shows a very simple example of the three layers painted onto the Landscape.

You should very quickly see a limitation with our approach thus far, the layers and textures look very flat, and it's hard to see any of the smaller details. Let's hop back into the Material Editor to improve our Materials Tiling.

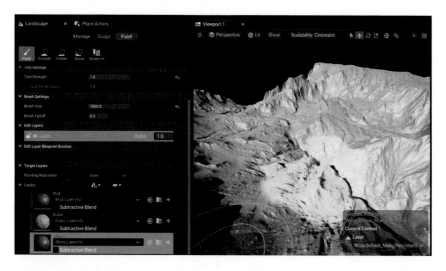

**FIGURE 4.4**   Test painting.

1. Using the **Content Browser** open the **Material M_Landscape** material, which is located in **Content | Materials | Master**.
2. Make some space to the left of the **Texture Sample** nodes, Right Click in the **Material Graph** and search for the *Landscape Layer Coords* node. This node is responsible for mapping of the Landscape Actor. Using the **Details** Panel, set the **Mapping Scale** to *4096*.
3. Now create a *Multiply* node by holding M and Left Clicking in the graph.
4. Connect the **Landscape Layer Coords** node into the **A** input of the **Multiply** node.
5. Underneath the **Multiply** node, create a Scalar Parameter by holding S and Left Clicking in the graph. Label this new node *Tiling* and set its **Default Value** to *200*.
6. Lastly, connect the **Tiling** node to the **B** input of the **Multiply** node.
7. We finally need to connect the **Output** pin of the **Multiply** node into each of the **UV Input** pins of the three **Texture Samples**.
8. Once this is done, Save your Material. An example of this Material can be seen in Figure 4.5.

If you preview the Landscape in the World, you should now see some textural detail. We've created a very simple tiling system that affords us the ability to repeat the textures easily to ensure they map well to the Landscape. Figure 4.6 shows the final result of this Material when applied to the landscape.

In some cases, the simple material we've created might suffice, but you are likely to require many more features to ensure your Landscape is decorated nicely. We may wish to add a wider variety of textures such as Normals and Roughness maps or as discussed early, we might want very specific controls to look at Height or Slopes. To build in more complexity, we are going to explore the usage of Material

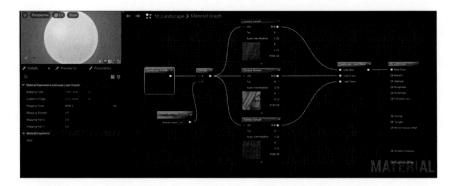

**FIGURE 4.5**   M_Landscape tiling control.

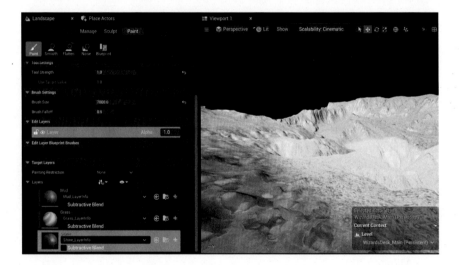

**FIGURE 4.6**   M_Landscape tiling in the viewport.

Functions. The idea is that we can create a specification of a Landscape Layer and then use it for all other Layers.

## Material Functions for Landscape Layers

Material Functions are an Unreal Asset that allows us to create reusable bits of Material Logic. The main benefit of building Material Functions is that they allow us to construct libraries of instantly available logic, which increases speed and consistency across projects. The types of nodes we use are a little different in Material Functions, we'll explore how we can create Inputs and link Functions to our Landscape Layer Process.

To begin this next part of the chapter, we are going to review what features all Landscape Layers might need. So far, we have created the ability to apply a Base

Color texture and tile it. Let's now look at the different features and explore how these features might benefit the Landscape Layer.

## Ingredients for Our Landscape Layer Material Function

The main focus of our Landscape Layer Material Function will be the incorporation of Textures. In our project, there are five types of potential Texture Inputs; these are Base Color, Specular, Roughness, Normal and Height. In your own projects, you may also require Ambient Occlusion, Displacement and World Position Offset. The function we build here is not all encompassing. take what we look at, and make it your own. Let's now review the five inputs we will be using.

1. **Base Color** – This input is typically a RGB Texture Sample created in another DCC. The Base Color input will need tiling control and consideration for Color Tinting and Repetition avoidance. Color Tinting will allow us to subtly change the color of our landscape, for example, make Grass slightly warmer in tone. Repetition avoidance allows us to break up a texture's appearance so it doesn't tile so visibly.

2. **Specular** – Unreal's default Specular value is 0.5, we should allow at least a Scalar Parameter Value Input, but some systems may use a channel or texture to give greater control. If you do use a channel or texture base solution you will need to incorporate tiling control and repetition avoidance like the Base Color pass.

3. **Roughness** – Typically, an artist will create a texture to dictate the Roughness input. It will require tiling control and repetition avoidance. In addition, it's useful to have a Linear Interpolation between a Minimum and Maximum value to control the overall Roughness.

4. **Normal** – As per roughness textures, we will need to adjust tiling on the Normal map. It's likely we'll also want a second Normal input to control Detail Normals. Landscapes and objects often blend a second Normal when up close.

5. **Height** – A height input is used for two main things, blending overall Landscape Layers or guiding Displacement. Both options require tiling control, in the example, we'll use Height to help blend our Materials.

Over the five inputs, we have common requirements such as Tiling Control are required for all inputs but some functionality such as that found in Roughness and Normal inputs can be quite bespoke. We'll now move onto making our Material Function to demonstrate some of the above in action.

## Building Our Landscape Layer Material Function

1. Navigate to **Content | Materials** folder using the Content Browser. Create a new **Folder** using the Right Click menu inside of the **Materials** folder and select **New Folder**. Label the new folder *Functions*.

2. Make sure you are inside the **Functions** folder, then Right Click and from the Menu select **Material | Material Function**. Label the new Material Function *MF_LandscapeLayer.*

3. Double click on **MF_LandscapeLayer** to open up the **Material Function Editor.**

4. The **Material Function Editor** is very similar to the **Material Editor** but straight away, you'll see the material output node, which is normally labeled with the materials name, has been replaced with an **Output Result** node. The **Output Result** node is the main way of passing data from a Material Function to the regular Material Editor. We can pass single parameter values or entire Material Attributes. For this example, **Right Click** to the left of the **Output Result** node and search for *Make Material Attributes* from the Menu.

5. Connect the **Make Material Attributes** node to the **Output Results** node.

6. We are now going to create the logic for the **BaseColor** input of the **Make Material Attributes** node. Make some space to the left of the **Make Material Attributes** node, Right Click and search for *Function Input*. By default, an **Input** node is set to a Vector 3 type which is perfect for setting Red, Green, and Blue values or loading color textures.

7. Select the **Input In** node and set its **Input Name** to *Base Color* and also *enable* **Use Preview Value as Default**.

8. Right Click to the left of our **Input Base Color (Vector 3)** node and search for *Texture Sample* from the Menu. Select the **Texture Sample** node and set the **Texture** value to *Landscape_Stone_BaseColor.* Next, Connect the **Texture Sample** node to the **Preview** pin of the **Base Color** input node.

9. Hold M and Left Click in front of the **Input Base Color (Vector 3)** node to create a **Multiply** node. Connect the output of the **Input Base Color (Vector 3)** node into the **B** input of the **Multiply** node.

10. Above the **A** Input of the **Multiply** node, Right Click and search for a *FunctionInput* node. Select the new **Input In** Node and set its **Input Name** to *Base Color Tint* and also *enable* **Use Preview Value as Default**.

11. To the left of the **Input Base Color Tint (Vector 3)** node, hold 3 on the keyboard and Left Click to create a Constant 3 Vector. We'll use this to create a temporary tint value. Select the Constant 3 Vector and set its **Constant Value** in the **Details** Panel to an RGB value of White *(1, 1, 1).*

12. Connect the Constant 3 Vector output to the **Preview** pin of the **Input Base Color Tint (Vector 3)** node.

13. Connect the output of the **Input Base Color Tint (Vector 3)** node to the **A** input of **Multiply** node.

14. Connect the output of the **Multiply** node to the **BaseColor** pin of the **Make Material Attributes**. You can review what our Function should look like so far in Figure 4.7.

We are now going to add controls for the specularity and roughness into the Material Function. This gives us the ability to tweak how the Landscape Material interacts with

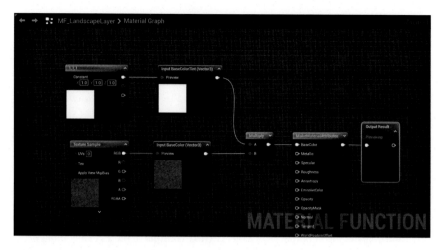

**FIGURE 4.7** Material function base color preview.

level lighting, allowing us to set precisely how rough or smooth a Landscape Layer should be. Roughness maps are very important textures, the Linear Interpolation Node will allow you to easily tweak roughness strength, let's get started!

1. Let's make a Scalar input for the **Specular** Attribute. To do this Move underneath the color nodes, hold **1** on your keyboard and Left Click to create a constant node. Set the **Default Value** of the constant to be *0.5* (default specular value in Unreal Materials).

2. To the right of the constant, Right Click and search the menu for a *Function Input* node.

3. Set the **Input Name** to *Specular* and set the **Input Type** to *Function Input Scalar*. Enable **Use Preview Value** as *Default*.

4. Now connect the output of the constant node into the **Preview** pin of the **Input Specular (Scalar)** node. Lastly, connect the output of the **Input Specular (Scalar)** node into the **Specular** pin of the **Make Material Attributes** node.

5. We are now going to build some nodes to help us control the Roughness of our Layers. Make some space under the Specular Nodes then hold 1 and Left Click twice to create two constant Nodes. Leave one of the **Constant** Nodes at a value of *0* and set the other to be a value of *1*.

6. Next, Right Click and create a *FunctionInput* Node. Set the **Input Name** to be *RoughnessMin* and set the **Input Type** to *Function Input Scalar*. Lastly, enable **Use Preview Value** as *Default*. Now connect the output of our **0** constant node into this **Input RoughnessMin (Scalar)** node.

7. Underneath, Right Click again, and from the menu, create a *FunctionInput* node. Set the **Input Name** to be *RoughnessMax* and set the **Input Type** to *Function Input Scalar*. Lastly, enable **Use Preview Value** as *Default*. Now connect the output of our **1** constant node into this **Input RoughnessMin (Scalar)** node.

8. To the right of the roughness input nodes, create a Linear Interpolate (**Lerp**) node by holding down L and Left Clicking. Connect the **Input RoughnessMin (Scalar)** node into the **A** slot of the **Lerp** node and connect the **Input RoughnessMax (Scalar)** node into the **B** slot of the **Lerp** node. This will allow us to tweak the Roughness values of any Landscape Layer.

9. Now Right Click in the **Material Graph** and select another *FunctionInput* node from the menu. Connect this node into the **Alpha** input of the **Lerp** node. Next, Select the **Input In** Node, set its **Input Name** to *RoughnessMask*, and set its **Input** Type to *Function Input Scalar*. Also, enable **Use Preview Value as Default**.

10. We now need to feed a default value into the **Input RoughnessMask (Scalar)** node, in this project, all Landscape textures use the Green Channel to store Roughness data. We can set this up by holding T and Left Clicking in the Material Graph. Then set the **Texture** to be *Landscape_Stone_ORM* and connect the **G** output pin of the **Texture Sample** to the **Preview** input of the **Input RoughnessMask (Scalar)** node.

11. Connect the **Output** of the **Lerp** node into the **Roughness** pin of the **Make Material Attributes** node.

12. You can compare the progress of your Material Function against Figure 4.8, the exact positioning of nodes isn't too important as long as it's relatively tidy and readable. You might find adding comments to sections of the graph is helpful to point out what each bit does. If you want to do this, select around any nodes you want to label and press C, a box will then be drawn where you can enter a Text Comment.

We are now going to create our Normal map logic for the Material Function. We shall create the ability to swap Normal maps and Detail Normal maps to help add depth to our Landscape Layers. Let's begin!

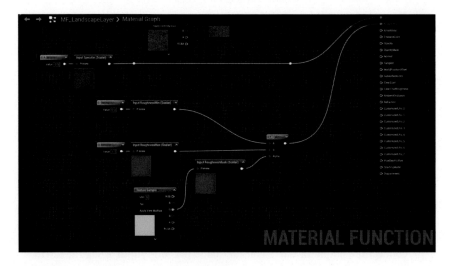

**FIGURE 4.8** Material function roughness preview.

1. To start, make some space underneath the Specular and Roughness logic, then hold T and Left Click twice to create two **Texture Sample** nodes. Move one of the **Texture Sample** nodes below the other and set both of the **Texture** Values to *Landscape_Stone_Normal*.

2. Next to the upper **Texture Sample**, Right Click in the Material Graph and Search for a *Function Input* node. Set the **Input Name** to *Normal*, leave the **Input Type** as the Default Value and enable **Use Preview Value as Default**. Lastly, connect the **Texture Sample RGB** pin to the **Preview** pin on the **Input Normal (Vector 3)** node.

3. Next to the lower **Texture Sample**, Right Click the Material Graph and Search for a *Function Input* Node. Set the **Input Name** to *DetailNormal*, leave the **Input Type** as the Default Value and enable **Use Preview Value as Default**. Lastly, connect the **Texture Sample RGB Output** to the **Preview** pin on the **Input Detail Normal (Vector 3)** node.

4. To the right of the **Input Normal (Vector 3)** node, Right Click and search for the *Blend Angle Corrected Normals* node. This node will blend the Normal and Detail Normals together properly. Connect the **Input Normal (Vector 3)** output into the **Base Normal (V3)** input of the **BlendAngleCorrectedNormals** node.

5. To the right of the **Input Details Normal (Vector 3)** node, Right Click and search for the *Flatten Normal* Node. The **FlattenNormal** node allows us to control the contrast/visibility of tiling detail noise which is great to add to prevent Normals from getting over the top. Connect the **Result** output of the **FlattenNormal** node into the **Additional Normal (V3)** input of the **BlendAngleCorrectedNormals** Node.

6. Connect the **Result** of the **BlendAngleCorrectedNormals** Node into the **Normal** pin of the **Make Materials Attribute** node.

7. Moving back to the **FlattenNormal** node, we now need to set up a bit of logic to control the **Flatness**. First hold 1 and Left Click to create a constant. A **Default Value** of *0* will add no **Flatness** to the **Detail Normal**. You can think of this as full intensity; a value of *1* will make the texture invisible/flat. Some artists like to invert this using a **OneMinus** node however the choice is really up to you, in the visual example of Figure 4.9, we have left the default value at 1 which in effect disables the **Detail Normal**.

8. After placing the constant, Right Click and search for a *Function Input* Node. Set the **InputName** to be *DetailNormalFlatness*, set the **Input Type** to be *Function Input Scalar* and enable **Use Preview Value as Default**. Now connect the constant to the **Preview** pin of the **Input DetailNormalFlatness (Scalar)** node and lastly, connect the **Output** of the **Input DetailNormalFlatness (Scalar)** node to the **Flatness** pin of the **FlattenNormal** node.

9. You can review the Normal logic by viewing Figure 4.9.

Let's now look at how we can add further Outputs to a Function. We have one already at the top which will export all of the **Make Material Attributes** values via an **Output Result** Node, however, what if we want something bespoke?

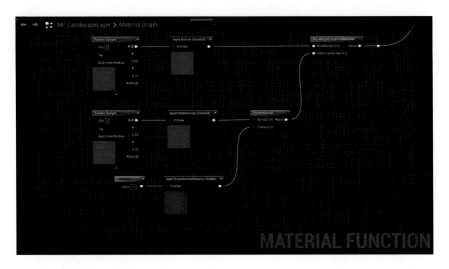

**FIGURE 4.9**   Material function normal preview.

1. To create something bespoke, Right Click just underneath the **Make Material Attributes** node and search for a *Function Output* node. Select the new node and set **Output Name** to be *Height*. We'll use this later to help blend textures.
2. Locate the **TextureSample** connected to the **Input RoughnessMask (Scalar)**. Connect the **B** pin of the **Texture Sample** to the **Output Height** node.

We can populate this Output much like any of the other Make Material input pins we've discussed in this chapter so far. It really depends on your team's workflow, for example, you could decide that all Blue Channels in Landscape Texture Masks have Height Data, or you could create a separate texture entirely, whichever route you go keep it consistent. You can see an example of this in Figure 4.10.

An overall shot of the Material Function so far can be seen in Figure 4.11, the exact positioning of the Nodes isn't important. Like mentioned previously, just try your best to keep things tidy.

The last feature we are going to explore for our Function is tiling breakup. On large landscapes, we want a mechanism to break up the Base Color a little or subtly change patterns. In this chapter, we will explore adding a bit of noise to the Base Color, however, you might also wish to look at Epic's Texture Bombing Function as an alternative. Texture Bombing changes how a texture is tiled quite dramatically, however, it can be fairly expensive depending on setup. We suggest starting with a simple noise system and then trying Epic's Texture Bombing Function to progress your knowledge later.

To get started, navigate to the top of the Material Function just above the Base Color logic to build our additions:

1. Right Click in the Material Graph and search for the *Texture Coordinate* Node. Once placed, create a duplicate of the **Texture Coordinate** node (CTRL+D) and place it underneath the first one. Select the upper **Texture Coordinate** node and set the **UTiling** And **VTiling** to *0.28*, then select the lower **Texture Coordinate** Node and set the **UTiling** and **VTiling** to *0.00025*. The idea here is that we'll use a Noise Texture at different scales to create a cool blend.

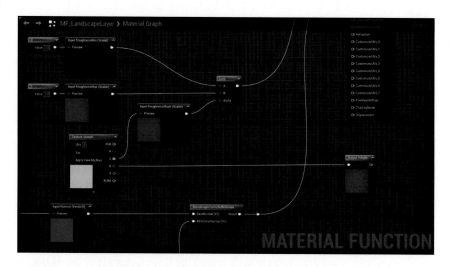

**FIGURE 4.10** Material function height output preview.

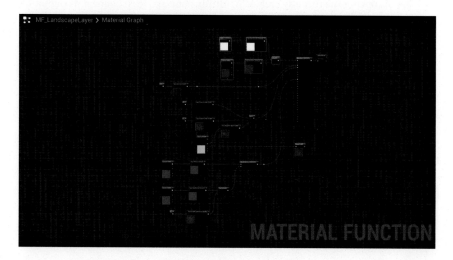

**FIGURE 4.11** Material function overall preview 1.

2. Next, place two **Texture Sample** nodes next to the **Texture Coordinate** nodes. You can do this by holding T and Left Clicking in the **Material Graph**. You may use any grayscale Noise you wish for the **Texture Value**, in the example, we utilized *TilingNoise05*, which is found in the **Engine | Content | MapTemplates** folder. To view Engine Content, click the COG icon when the search menu is open, and enable the property **Show Engine Content**. Set both **Texture Sample** nodes to use your chosen noise texture and also set the **Sampler Source** to *Shared Wrap*.

3. When both of the **Texture Sample** nodes are setup, create a **Multiply** node to the right of them by holding M and Left Clicking in the Material Graph. Connect the **R** pin of the upper **Texture Sample** into the **A** input of the

**Multiply** node and connect the **R** output from the lower **Texture Sample** into the **B** input of the **Multiply** node.

4. Next, create a **Lerp** node, by holding L and Left Clicking in the Material Graph. Connect the output of the **Multiply** node into the **Alpha** pin of the **Lerp** node.

5. Next create a constant node just above the upper **Texture Sample**, you can do this by holding 1 and Left Clicking in the Graph. Set the constants **Value** to around *0.6*.

6. Now right click in the Material Graph and search for a *Function Input* Node. Set the **Input Name** to *ColorNoiseTint*, set the **Input Type** as the *FunctionInputScalar* and enable **Use Preview Value as Default**. Connect the output of the **Input ColorNoiseTint (Scalar)** node into the **A** input of the **Lerp** node.

7. Lastly, create a **Multiply** node by holding M and Left Clicking in Material Graph. Connect the output of the **Lerp** node into the **A** input of the **Multiply** node. Then Move the **Multiply** node near to the **Base Color** pin of the **Make Material Attributes** node. Connect the existing **Multiply** node's output into the **B** input of the recently created **Multiply** node and then connect its output pin into the **BaseColor** pin of the **Make Material Attributes** node.

8. Figure 4.12 shows the construction of the repetition logic, by adjusting the Scalar we will be able to subtly add a bit of noise on top of the Base Color Texture. Figure 4.13 shows an example of our final Function, which will be useful for checking these final connections.

The Function we've created is just the beginning. Once you begin mastering this process, you may wish to look into incorporating Ambient Occlusion, Parallax Occlusion Mapping and Texture Bombing to further consolidate the Landscape Features. To test what we've made, you can now drag and drop our Material Function into any

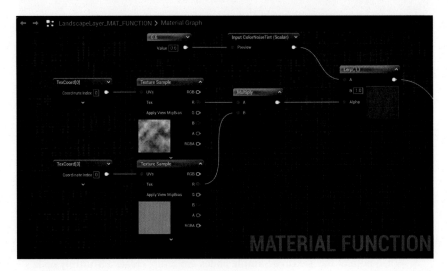

**FIGURE 4.12**    Material function repetition breakup preview.

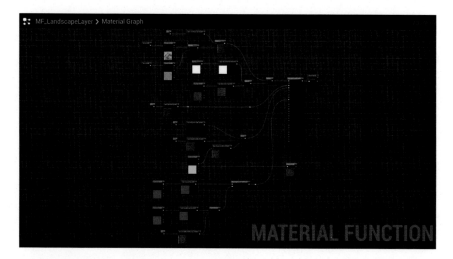

**FIGURE 4.13** Material function overall preview 2.

**FIGURE 4.14** Material function drag and drop preview.

other Material. After dragging and dropping our Material Function from the Content Browser into a Material, a special Material Function Node will appear that matches the one shown in Figure 4.14. In Chapter 5, we'll explore how to use this to create our Layered Landscape Material.

## Conclusion

In this chapter, we've explored the ingredients of Landscape Materials and Landscape Material Functions. We created our very first simple Landscape Material before going on to create a Material Function to help us speed up the process of texturing our landscape. Material Functions are an amazingly powerful part of Unreal Material creation and once you've begun to utilize them, you'll find them a helpful part of development in all material creation.

In Chapter 5, we'll begin to explore how to create a fully layered Landscape Material that utilizes our Material Function. But before we do, let's review this chapter's quiz.

## Chapter 4  Quiz

Question 1: What is a Landscape Material?

a. A Landscape Material is a bespoke material that is applied to any floor mesh in Unreal.

b. A Landscape Material allows us to sculpt a Landscape Actor.

c. A Landscape Material is a bespoke material that is applied to a Landscape Actor in Unreal.

Question 2: What are Landscape Layer Blends Used?

a. Landscape Layer Blends controls the overall height of our terrain in Unreal.

b. Landscape Layer Blends allows us to blend together different types of surfaces in Unreal such as Rock, Grass and Stone.

c. Landscape Layer Blends control how our Landscape Blends with other level geometry.

Question 3: How do we paint our Landscape Material onto the Landscape Actor?

a. We need to run a procedural Landscape actor to paint our Landscape Material.

b. We need to apply a Landscape Material onto a Landscape Actor and then select Layers to Paint using the Landscape Mode.

c. We need to use the Mesh Paint Mode to assign vertex colors to paint our Landscape Material.

Question 4: Why is it important to control the tiling of textures in a Landscape Material?

a. We can often see Landscapes up close and at distance, we want to be able to control the tiling of textures to ensure that at multiple draw distances, the Landscape looks good.

b. We need textures to tile a lot to be more memory efficient.

c. Tiling allows us to place mortar seams in between texture samples.

## Answers

Question 1: c

Question 2: b

Question 3: b

Question 4: a

# 5

## Creating Layered Landscape Materials

### Introduction to Layered Landscape Materials

This chapter introduces you to the Material Creation for your Landscapes, you'll learn about:

- What Layered Landscape Materials are?
- What we use Landscape Materials for?
- How to construct your own Landscape Material?
- How to begin painting Landscape Materials in Unreal?

But where do we begin? We are first going to explore a key ingredient of a Layered Landscape Material, a Material Function.

### Using Material Functions to Create Landscape Layers

Material Functions are an Unreal Asset that allows us to create reusable bits of Material Logic. In Chapter 4, we set up a Function that can easily be adapted for Landscape Layers with lots of inputs to offer artists flexibility. We can use functions like this in a couple of ways:

1. To separate Material Functions that represent the different surfaces of a Landscape. For example, a Material Function for Grass, Sand, Rock and Snow. This approach is useful if you are likely to reuse layers or have a game world with lots of different locations.
2. To customize the Material Function within a Master Material. This is similar but in effect all the setup is done in one place. In this chapter, we'll go with this approach as it's a simple starting point, however we recommend you also look into option A if you work on a project with many Landscapes.

Let's now build our Material Function.

### Adding Our Material Function

1. You can continue with either of the levels from Chapter 4. If you wish to work with the provided files we recommend using the **Landscape_Material_ Start** level.

DOI: 10.1201/9781032663883-5

2. Navigate to the **Materials | Master** folder in the **Content Browser**.

3. Double click on our **M_Landscape** material.

4. Drag select over all existing nodes and hit the delete key. This will allow us to start from scratch.

5. There are a few ways we can add our Material Function to the Material Graph. We can:

   - Right Click in the Material Graph and search for *Material Function Call*. You can then use the **Details** panel to set the **Material Function Parameter** to *MF_LandscapeLayer* via a drop-down menu.

   - In the **MF_LandscapeLayer** Material Function, if we enable the property **Expose to Library** and Save, you can then Right Click on any part of the Material Editor Graph and search for *MF_LandscapeLayer* instead of using the Material Function Call Node.

   - Drag and Drop the **MF_LandscapeLayer** (or any other material function) from the **Content Browser** onto the Material Editor Graph. I often resort to this option as there's less typing involved but there's no right or wrong way.

6. Once you have one of the **Material Functions** placed in the Material Editor, make sure there is plenty of room between the Material Result node and Duplicate the Material Function so there are four copies, ready for setting up each of our layers: Grass, Mud, Stone and River Mud.

7. Arrange the copies so they are stacked vertically with plenty of room around them. Figure 5.1 shows what things will look at a zoomed-out level and Figure 5.2 will show all of the inputs we now need to set up per layer.

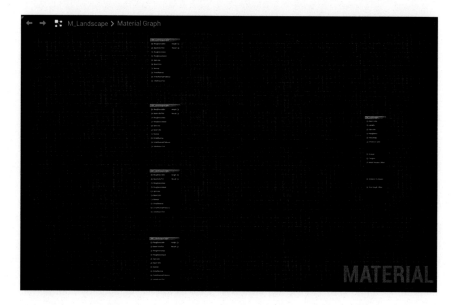

**FIGURE 5.1** Layered material overview.

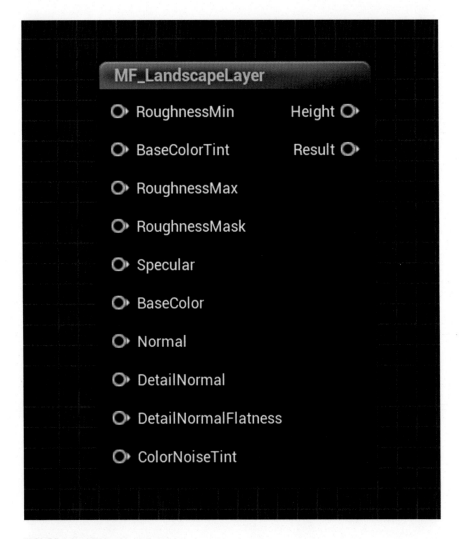

**FIGURE 5.2** MF landscape layer.

With the Material Functions placed, we can move onto tailoring the specific Landscape layers and add in the correct Textures and Parameters.

### Creating Mud, Grass, Stone and River Mud

In this section, we'll begin to set up our Material Layers by adding inputs to the four Material Functions. We are going to work from top to bottom, once one of the Functions is set up, it makes it easier to complete the others as we use Duplicate/Copy and Paste to complete the others. To begin, make sure you have the M_Landscape material open and scroll to the top most **MF_LandscapeLayer** node by holding the right mouse button down and dragging the mouse.

1. An easy way to create all the parameters we need is to sequentially move down the list of inputs and Right Click. When the options menu appears select **Promote to Parameter**. This will automatically label and create the right parameter for the function in most situations. Where it will fail is when we want to use a Texture, to avoid this go down the list and use this approach for the following inputs: **RoughnessMin**, **BaseColorTint**, **RoughnessMax**, **Specular, DetailNormalFlatness** and **Color Noise Tint.**

2. When you've promoted the initial Parameters, you should see something like the example in Figure 5.3. One of the side effects of the **Promote to Parameter** option is that Unreal adds the input type to the name of Parameter for example **(S)** for **Scalar**. You can remove these if you wish by editing the Parameter Names in the **Detail** panel.

3. Next, we need to create the inputs for the remaining four texture inputs. To do this, hold T and Left Click in the Material Graph, this will create a **Texture Sample** node. Right Click on the **Texture Sample** and select **Convert to Parameter**, this will convert the **Texture Sample** to a **TextureSampleParameter2D**. We can now select the **TextureSampleParameter2D** with Left Click and use Copy and Paste three times to create the other three missing Parameters. Be sure to edit the **Parameter Name** on each **TextureSampleParameter2D** to match the Material Function Input, for example, *RoughnessMask, BaseColor, Normal* and *DetailNormal*. When connecting the **TextureSampleParameter2D**'s to the **MF_LandscapeLayer** node, use the **RGB** output for **BaseColor, Normal** and **Detail Normal** Inputs. For the **Roughness Mask** input, only use the **Green Channel**. This is because the Roughness Textures use different channels for other scale inputs such as Ambient Occlusion and or Height.

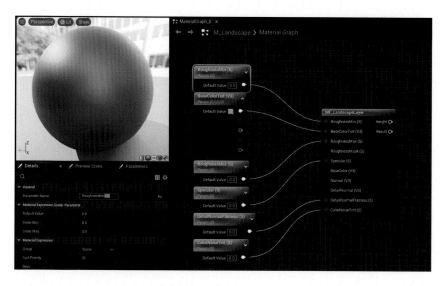

**FIGURE 5.3** MF landscape layer example inputs.

4. We've now got a function setup with the correct parameters but with "empty"/ default values. We have to go through each one of the Function Inputs and ensure the property is correct.

5. **RoughnessMin** can stay at a value of *0*. This represents the lowest roughness our Function can go to. Lastly, using the **Details** panel, edit the **Parameter Name** to read as *MudRoughnessMin* and type *Mud* into the Group. We'll do this to each Parameter so they are aligned to one of the Landscape Layers (Grass, Mud, Stone and River Mud).

6. **BaseColorTint** needs to change to a value of *1* in each channel, which will make it white. The default value of white will have no tinting effect; it's like setting the value to off. Lastly, using the Details panel, edit the **Parameter Name** to read as *MudBaseColorTint* and type *Mud* into the **Group**.

7. **RoughnessMax** needs to change to a value of *1*. This represents the highest roughness our Function can go to. Use the **Details** panel to edit the **Parameter Name** to read as *MudRoughnessMax* and type *Mud* into the **Group**.

8. **RoughnessMask** needs its texture assignment. Use the Details panel to set the **RoughnessMask Texture** to *Textures | Landscape | Landscape_Mud_ ORM*, edit the **Parameter Name** to read as *MudRoughnessMask* and type *Mud* into the **Group**.

9. **Specular** needs to change to a value of *0.5*, which is the default in Unreal. You could also use a Texture here if further detail/control is required. Use the **Details** panel to edit the **Parameter Name** to read as *MudSpecular* and type *Mud* into the **Group**.

10. **BaseColor** needs its texture assignment. Use the **Details** panel to set the **BaseColor Texture** to *Textures | Landscape | Landscape_Mud_BaseColor*, edit the **Parameter Name** to read as *MudBaseColor* and type *Mud* into the **Group**.

11. **Normal** needs its texture assignment. Use the **Details** panel to set the **Normal Texture** to *Textures | Landscape | Landscape_Mud_Normal*, edit the **Parameter Name** to read as *MudNormal* and type *Mud* into the **Group**.

12. **DetailNormal** needs its texture assignment. Use the **Details** panel to set the **Normal Texture** to *Textures | Landscape | Landscape_Mud_Normal*, edit the **Parameter Name** to read as *MudDetailNormal* and type *Mud* into the **Group**.

13. **DetailNormalFlatness** needs to change to a value of *1*. A value of 1 will make the **Detail Normal** fully flat/have no effect. A value of 0 will have a lot of additional detail, I find it's helpful to have materials in the off position to begin with until you decide how much contrast or surface information you want to see. Use the **Details** panel to edit the **Parameter Name** to read as *MudDetailNormalFlatness* and type *Mud* into the Group.

14. **ColorNoiseTint** needs to change to a value of *0.7*. This will add some subtle noise to the albedo. The exact value is completely up to you, tweak and have fun. Use the **Details** panel to also edit the **Parameter Name** to read as *MudColorNoiseTint* and type *Mud* into the **Group**.

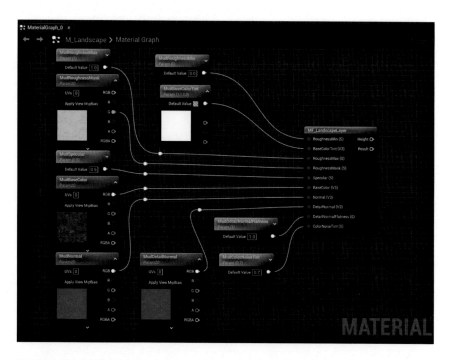

**FIGURE 5.4**   Mud MF landscape layer.

15. Figure 5.4 shows the completed Mud Landscape Layer. Some of the input lines have been adjusted by double clicking to add **Reroute** nodes (little circles on the Material line connections). This creates tidier diagrams for print but you might also like to use these for keeping your Material Graphs readable.

Each tiling texture used in a **Landscape Material** requires its Sampler Source to be set to Shared: Wrap. This will prevent your **Landscape Material** from running out of Texture Samples too soon (Default is 16 without Wrap). Be sure to revisit the **Base Color**, **Normal**, **ORM** and **Detail Normal Texture Sample Parameters** and update their **Sampler Source** as shown in Figure 5.5. You'll know if you haven't done this as Unreal will randomly stop rendering parts of your terrain and replace the Texture information with the missing texture material.

At this point, you might also like to select the nodes and press C to add a text Comment. This helps you identify parts of the Material, this becomes important as things become more complex. Figure 5.6 shows this in effect and also shows what the Function might look like if we didn't use **Parameters** for **Texture Inputs**.

From here, we now need to complete the remaining Landscape Layers for Grass, Stone and River Mud. The process is identical to what we've just followed, however, when creating these values make sure that you do not have Parameters that share the exact same name, doing this will cause conflicts and only allow for one Parameter value to exist. This is why we used the additional text "Mud" on the previous parameters.

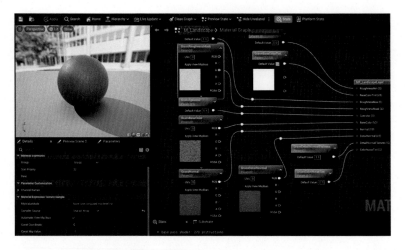

**FIGURE 5.5** Texture sample sampler source.

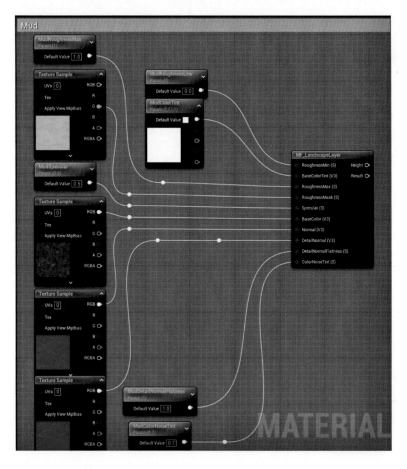

**FIGURE 5.6** Mud MF landscape layer.

To begin work on the Grass **MF_LandscapeLayer** set up you may find it easier to select all of the **Mud** nodes and use Copy and Paste to create a copy of all nodes. We now need to customize these nodes to reflect Grass, Stone and River Mud.

1. After copying and pasting the **Mud** nodes, go through each of the duplicated Parameters and replace the **Mud** text with *Grass* and set the **Group** to *Grass* using the **Details** panel.
2. Now we need to set the Textures, Select the **GrassRoughnessMask** node and set the **Texture** to *Textures | Landscape | Landscape_Grass_ORM.*
3. Next, select the **GrassBaseColor** node and set the **Texture** to *Textures | Landscape | Landscape_Grass_BaseColor.*
4. For both **GrassNormal** and **GrassDetailNormal**, set the **Texture** to *Textures | Landscape | Landscape_Grass_Normal.*
5. The setup process this time around is much faster, to review the Grass please examine Figure 5.7, and for a brief zoomed out shot, please check Figure 5.8.

Now, we need to create the Stone set up following the same process.

1. Select the **Grass** nodes and Copy and Paste them. You will now need to repeat the steps above but for **Stone**.
2. After copying and pasting the **Grass** nodes, go through each of the duplicated **Parameters** and replace the **Grass** text with *Stone* and set the **Group** to *Stone* using the **Details** panel.

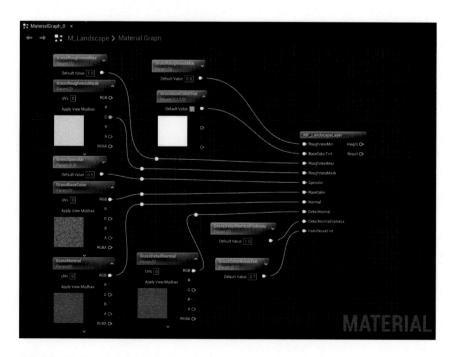

**FIGURE 5.7** Grass MF landscape layer.

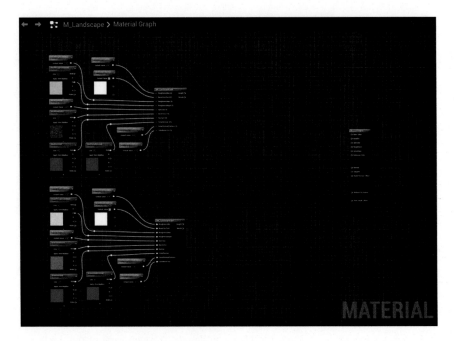

**FIGURE 5.8**  MF landscape layers overview.

3. Now, we need to set the **Textures**, Select the **StoneRoughnessMask** node and set the **Texture** to *Textures | Landscape | Landscape_Stone_ORM*.

4. Next, select the **StoneBaseColor** node and set the **Texture** to *Textures | Landscape | Landscape_Stone_BaseColor.*

5. For both **StoneNormal** and **StoneDetailNormal,** set the Texture to *Textures | Landscape | Landscape_Stone_Normal.*

6. The setup process this time around is much faster, to review the Stone, please review Figure 5.9.

We have one last layer to create, which is the River Mud. Select the previous Mud nodes and use Copy and Paste to create a copy of all of these nodes.

1. After copying and pasting the **Mud** nodes, go through each of the duplicated **Parameters** and replace the **Mud** text with *RiverMud* and set the Group to *RiverMud* using the **Details** panel.

2. Select the node **RiverMudSpecular** and set its value to *1.*

3. Select the node **RiverMudRoughnessMax** and set its value to *0.7.*

4. These two small tweaks will allow our **River Mud** layers to appear a bit wetter and darker than the standard **Mud** layer.

5. To review please check out Figure 5.10.

We have now set up the basic inputs for the four Landscape Layers, from here, we can begin to control how they blend together.

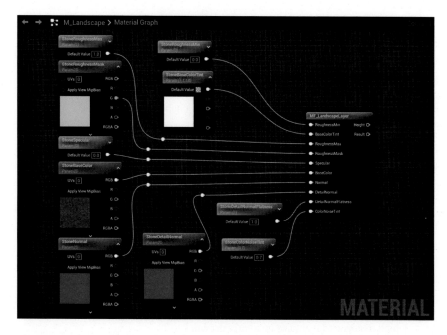

**FIGURE 5.9**    Stone MF landscape layer.

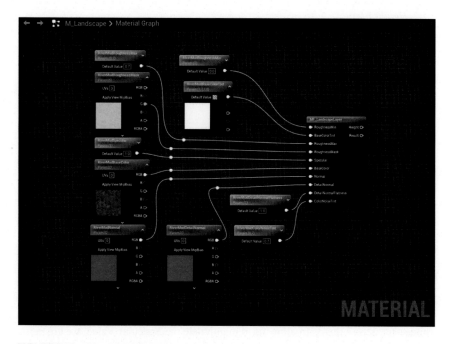

**FIGURE 5.10**    RiverMud MF landscape layer.

## Blending Landscape Layers

We are now going to begin blending our Layers together, this will work in a similar manner to Chapter 4. We'll start by adding a Landscape Layer Blend node and then connect in the results of the four Material Functions. For now, this Blend system will create paintable Landscape Layers, but in a later chapter, we'll take this further by adding automatic landscape painting.

To get started, make sure you have the **M_Landscape Material** open in the Material Editor.

1. Move to the right of the Material Functions, Right Click in the Material Graph and search for the *Landscape Layer Blend* node.
2. Select the **Landscape Layer Blend** node and move over to the **Details** panel. We now need to enter the amount of **Layers,** we wish to Blend. Click the + button next to **Layers** to create four array elements. This process starts counting at 0, so don't be surprised when it shows entries 0, 1, 2 and 3.
3. Select **Index 0**, set the **Layer Name** to *Mud*. Change the **Blend Type** to *LB Height Blend* and set the **Preview Weight** to *1*. This ensures that the first Index is visible, if you don't do this then you may have a black Landscape which means no layers are currently drawn.
4. Select **Index 1**, set the **Layer Name** to *Stone*. Change the **Blend Type** to *LB Height Blend*.
5. Select **Index 2**, set the **Layer Name** to *Grass*. Change the **Blend Type** to *LB Height Blend*.
6. Select **Index 3**, set the **Layer Name** to *RiverMud*. Change the **Blend Type** to *LB Height Blend*.
7. You can compare the setup against Figure 5.11.

We now need to connect our Functions to the Landscape Layer Blend:

1. Connect the **Height** and **Result** output pins of each **MF_LandscapeLayer** Function to the corresponding input of the **Landscape Layer Blend** node.
2. You will need to repeat this for each layer, the result should be as shown in Figure 5.12.

This process is made easier if all the functions and nodes are neatly aligned so that you can ensure a tidy flow in the Material graph. Once connected, we can now begin to build some early control for Specularity.

## Controlling Specularity

By default, Unreal Materials have a Specularity of 0.5 and little control for how it fades across a landscape. This can lead to landscapes looking like they have a soft white sheen across them. To allow us to manipulate the Specular Value, we are going to break apart the Landscape Blend and then join it back together, using Make and

**FIGURE 5.11** Landscape layer blend node properties.

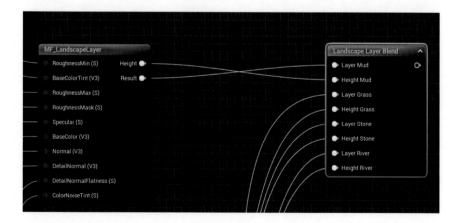

**FIGURE 5.12** Mud landscape layer function to landscape layer blend.

Break Material attributes. This approach is useful when we want to manipulate one or more properties of complex Materials.

Let's get started!!!

1. To the right of the **Landscape Layer Blend** node, Right Click in the Material Graph and search for *Make Material Attributes*.
2. To enable this node to connect to our Material Result node, deselect any nodes in the Material Graph, navigate to the **Details** panel and enable **Use Material Attributes**.
3. Connect the output of the **MakeMaterialAttributes** node into the **Material Attributes** input of the **Material Result** node, as shown in Figure 5.13.
4. Next, before the **MakeMaterialAttributes** node, Right Click and search for *BreakMaterialAttributes*. This node needs to be first connected to the output pin of the **Landscape Layer Blend** mode, Connect the output to the **Attr** input of the **BreakMaterialAttributes**.
5. Next, connect the following outputs from the **BreakMaterialAttributes** to the **Make Material Attributes**: **BaseColor**, **Roughness**, **Normal** and **AmbientOcclusion**. This ensures that these four values are passed along to the result of the Material and leaves us with the ability to alter the Specular Value.
6. Drag a connection out from the **Specular** pin of the **BreakMaterialAttributes** and from the pop-up menu, search for *Linear Interpolate*. You can also place the **Lerp** manually by holding L and Left Clicking.

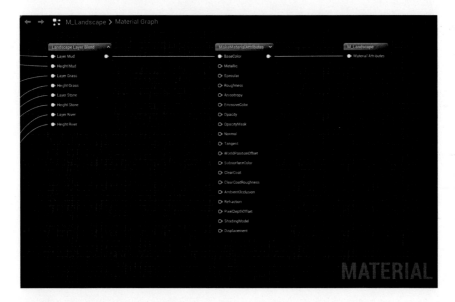

**FIGURE 5.13** Setting up Make Material attributes.

7. Move the **Lerp** node underneath the **BreakMaterialAttribute** and **MakeMaterialAttribute** nodes. Make sure the **Specular** output goes into the **B** input of the **Lerp** node. This will mean we can blend between a value of black (the **A** input) and then whatever is in the **Specular** of the Material Functions.

8. For the **Alpha** input of the **Lerp** node, create a **Scalar Parameter** by holding S and Left Clicking. Label the **Scalar Parameter** *Spec Contrast* using the **Details** panel. Set the **Default Value** to be *1*. We can use this to blend between the upper and lower values of specularity.

9. Next, create a **Multiply** node by holding M and Left Clicking in the Material Graph. Connect the output of the **Lerp** into the **A** input of the **Multiply**. Then create a **Scalar Parameter** by holding S and Left Clicking. Label the **Scalar Parameter** *Spec Strength* using the **Details** panel. Set the **Default Value** to be *1*. Connect this into the **B** input of the **Multiply**.

10. Connect the output of the **Multiply** into the **Specular** input of the **MakeMaterialAttributes**.

11. You can review our Specular tweaks in Figure 5.14.

We now have some control to adjust the amount of Specularity on our Landscape but we will revisit this piece shortly to add some additional control for Distance Fading. To be able to add Distance Fading, we are going to set up our Landscape with Runtime Virtual Textures in the next section.

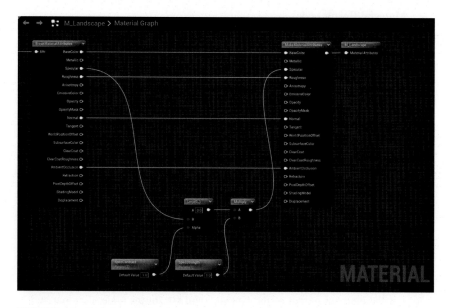

**FIGURE 5.14** Setting up specular control.

## Runtime Virtual Texturing for Landscapes

We introduced RVT as a useful technology in Chapter 4, their ability to create a cache for a large area is useful in addition to being able to blend art assets with landscape texturing. We are now going to explore how we can set up RVT in our Landscape Material but also manage the assets it requires within Unreal.

Landscape Runtime Virtual Textures require us to create volumes, which capture landscape information such as color and height. This data is then passed onto a Texture Asset in the Content Browser. We can then load this texture inside of an Unreal Material, which helps improve the performance of our Landscape Materials.

Once we have RVT working, we need to consider things such as distance scaling to ensure our Landscapes look great up close and far away.

Let's get building!

## Setting up Our RVT Material Links

The first piece of Material nodes we'll build will help us export/make available Material Channels to the RVT system. We have to tell Unreal what specific materials properties such as Base Color or Roughness are available for it to process in a volume. This piece of the graph is usually done at the end so that it can take in any previous shader logic. If you create these types of linking nodes too early, you can miss out on parts of your Landscape so try to wait until most of the Material is built before creating the nodes below.

1. Make a bit of room between the **MakeMaterialAttributes** node and the **Material Result** node.
2. Right Click in the Material Graph and search for the *GetMaterialAttributes* node. Connect the input of this node into the output of the **MakeMaterialAttributes** node.
3. Select the **GetMaterialAttributes** node and hover over to the **Details** panel. Create four Array Elements using the+button for the **Attribute Get Types**. Unreal will automatically populate the four Attributes, using the drop-down menu to change these values to:
   - **Base Color,**
   - **Specular,**
   - **Roughness,**
   - **Normal.**
4. Now Right Click in the **Material Graph** again and search for a *Runtime Virtual Texture Output* node.
5. Connect the first three outputs of the **GetMaterialAttributes** node (**Base Color**, **Specular** and **Roughness**) to the inputs of the **Runtime Virtual Texture Output** node.
6. For the **Normal** output of the **GetMaterialAttributes** node, drag out and from the menu search for the *Transform/TransformVector* node.
7. Select the **TransformVector** node and using the **Details** panel, change the **Source** to *Tangent Space* and the **Destination** to *World Space*. Then connect

the output pin of the **TransformVector** node into the **Normal** input pin on the **RuntimeVirtual Texture Output** node.

8. To populate the **Height** input of the **Runtime Virtual Texture Output** node, Right Click in the Material Graph and search for the *World Position* node.

9. Drag out from the **XYZ** output of the **World Position** node and search for the *Component Mask* node.

10. Select the **Mask (R G)** node and *enable* only the **B** channel, which is the height value of landscape.

11. Next, Connect the output of the **Mask (B)** node into the **Height** input of the **Runtime Virtual Texture Output** node.

12. We now need to populate the **Opacity** input, to do this create a **Constant** by holding 1 and Left Clicking in the Material Graph. Set the **Default Value** to be *1* (Fully Opaque).

13. We shall leave the **Mask** value unpopulated as we don't have anything to feed into the input yet.

14. We've now completed the RVT Output section of the Material, please review Figure 5.15 to compare your progress.

Now we have enabled our Material to broadcast its attributes to the RVT system we know we need to create some logic that will allow us to input the captured texture asset. This is where we can harvest some performance benefit from our hard work. The next few nodes will effectively replace the previous material nodes by using a RVT Texture Cache. Let's get making!

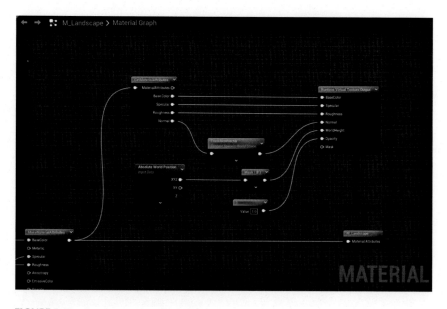

**FIGURE 5.15** Creating our material RVT output.

1. Right Click in the Material Graph just after the **MakeMaterialAttributes** node. From the pop-up menu, search for the node *Runtime Virtual Texture Sample*.
2. Right Click again in the Material Graph and search for the node *Make Material Attributes*.
3. Connect the following outputs from the **Runtime Virtual Texture Sample** to the **MakeMaterialAttributes** node:
   - **Base Color,**
   - **Specular,**
   - **Roughness,**
   - **Normal.**
4. Right Click once again in the **Material Graph** and search for the node *Virtual Texture Feature Switch*. Connect the Output from the original **MakeMaterial Attributes** node to the **No** input of the **VirtualTextureFeatureSwitch** and connect the output from the new **MakeMaterialAttributes** node to the **Yes** input of the **VirtualTextureFeatureSwitch**.
5. Finally, connect the output of the **VirtualTextureFeatureSwitch** to the **M_Landscape** Material Result node. You can review this series of nodes by looking at Figure 5.16.

The Feature Switch we've just created allows us to easily toggle between RVT-based Landscapes. Toggles like these are important because not all platforms are the same and support the same methodologies. We now need to build some assets that exist outside of the Material Editor and connect them to our Material.

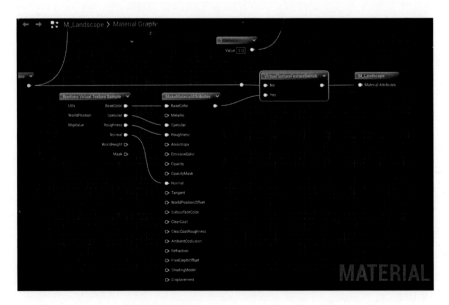

**FIGURE 5.16**   Creating our material RVT input.

## Setting up Virtual Texture Volumes and Drawing Virtual Textures

In this section, we'll need to jump around the editor a little bit to create assets and actors needed to power the RVT system. We'll begin by creating RVT Textures Assets that will help us capture information about our landscape. After this, we will make volumes that will process the Landscape before going back to our Material to finish up some Asset Linkage.

Let's begin creating our textures!

1. Select your Landscape Actor in the **World Outliner**. In the example scene, it will be called **Landscape**, however select whichever is the working Landscape in your level.

2. Next, using the **Details** panel, Scroll Down to the **Draw in Virtual Textures** property. Use the + button to create two assets.

3. Expand the DropDown for each index. You should get a pop-up menu, select the option at the top under **Create New Asset**, **Runtime Virtual Texture**.

4. Using the dialogue options save the first RVT Texture as *RVTColor* in the folder **Textures | Landscape**.

5. Repeat the process for the next Index and call this new RVT Texture, *RVT Height*.

6. Now Double Click on both Runtime Virtual Textures in the **Content Browser**. Set the **Virtual Texture Content** drop down of **RVTColor** to be **Base Color, Normal, Roughness** and **Specular** and set the **Virtual Texture Content** drop down of **RVTHeight** to be **World Height**.

7. The default **RVT Texture Sizes** are set to values of *8, 2* and *2*. We can increase these a little bit to *11, 3* and *2* for further resolution. This alteration raises the **Texture Size** in the tiles for further detail and raises the amount of each virtual texture tile. The size dimensions offer a good vantage point for optimisation, if you run into performance troubles, lower resolutions for size of the texture will help and a larger resolution of the tile itself can oddly help as the system updates less.

8. You can review these settings in Figures 5.17 and 5.18.

**FIGURE 5.17** Creating our landscape RVT textures.

**FIGURE 5.18** Configuring RVT texture options.

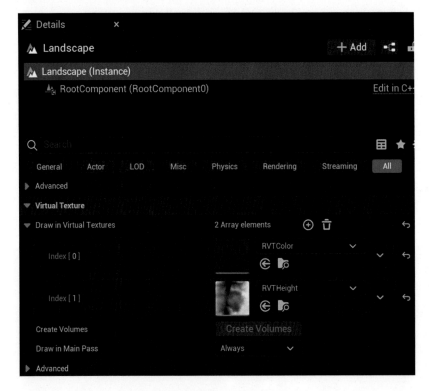

**FIGURE 5.19** Create RVT volume options.

Now our texture assets exist, go back to the Landscape Actor shown in Figure 5.19 and hit the button **Create Volumes**. This will create volumes for any RVT Texture setup in the Landscape, it will automatically size the volume to your Landscape and apply the texture!

If you ever need to adjust these volumes, you can search for them in the World Outliner with the term *RunTimeVirtualTextureVolume*. Hopefully, you will not need to adjust them, the most likely thing to adjust is the bounds, which should match your Landscape.

Let's now pop back to our Landscape Material:

1. Select the **Runtime Virtual Texture Sample** node.
2. Set its **Virtual Texture** property in the **Details** panel to be our recently created **RVTColor** texture.
3. At this point, your world may resemble Figure 5.20 if your Landscape was built initially with Material described in Chapter 4. Do not worry if not though as we still have plenty to finish.

We have now created the necessary assets to link the Actors and Materials together to help populate our RVT Textures. We now need to ensure our Material is applied correctly to our Landscape and then move on to some finishing touches to control tiling.

Let's now ensure our **Material** is applied correctly. We need to check that the Landscape is reading the Layer names properly and has info assets set up to help store their properties. Once this is done, we can move on to painting and further tweaking.

1. To finish our Landscape Material setup, select the Landscape Actor.
2. Ensure that the Landscape Actor has the **M_Landscape** material applied.
3. Next, change from **Selection Mode** to *Landscape Mode* using the top left UI.

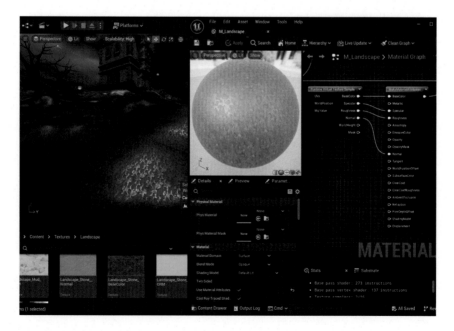

**FIGURE 5.20** Landscape preview.

**FIGURE 5.21**   Landscape layer setup.

4. Set the **Landscape** tab to *Paint Mode.*
5. Scroll down the UI until you see the **Layers** at the bottom. These should match those shown in Figure 5.21.
6. Make sure each layer has a **Layer Info** asset associated with it. You can use the + button next to each layer to make an asset if needed. All of the Layers should be **WeightBlended (Normal)** and should be saved into the **Maps | WizardsDesk | WizardsDesk_Main_sharedassets** folder. If you have previously completed Chapter 4, you will likely find that some of these are already completed.
7. Make sure each one is correct by reviewing against Figure 5.21.

You should now be able to paint the different layers onto the terrain using the standard painting tools. Select each layer and try using the Left Mouse Button, you may experience a little load time for the first click. You can easily fill or clear layers by Right Clicking if you want to make very significant changes. The Right Click option also gives you the ability to import a texture to control the layers blend, this is helpful if you want to make detailed erosion layers in packages like Houdini or World Machine. Figure 5.22 shows the different layers' effects on the Landscape.

We can now move on to controlling tiling and finessing our material!

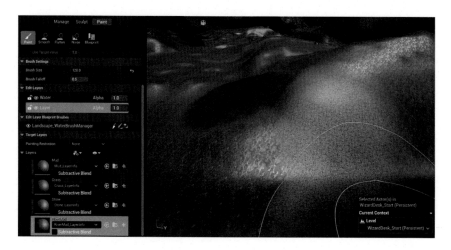

**FIGURE 5.22** Landscape layer example.

## Setting up Tiling and Fading Controls

For our final section, we are going to focus mostly on Tiling Control. We need to explore smart ways of managing lots of Texture UV changes to avoid the Material Graph from becoming too complex. To do this, we are going to leverage a recent feature in Unreal Engine which is the named reroute node. This feature allows us to build unconnected functionality quite far away in the Material Graph and not connections going everywhere around the screen.

Let's get started.

1. Move to the left of your Material Graph away from our existing nodes.
2. Right Click in the Material Graph and search for the *Landscape Layer Coords* node. Leave this node with its default settings.
3. Drag out from the **Landscape Coords** node three times and create three **Multiply** nodes, vertically stacked. For the **B** inputs in the **Multiply** nodes, we need to create three **Scalar Parameters**, create these by holding the S key and Left Clicking on the graph, label them *CloseTiling*, *DistanceTiling* and *DetailTiling*.
4. Set the value of **CloseTiling** to be *0.15*, **DistanceTiling** to be *0.05* and **DetailingTiling** to be *8*.
5. Next, drag out of the top **Multiply** and search for the *Named Reroute Declaration* node, call the first one *CloseTiling*.
6. Then, drag out of the middle **Multiply** and search for the *Named Reroute Declaration* node, call this one *DistanceTiling*.
7. Finally, drag out of the bottom **Multiply** and search for the *Named Reroute Declaration* node, call this final one, *DetailTiling*.
8. Figure 5.23 shows a quick breakdown of the nodes for comparison.

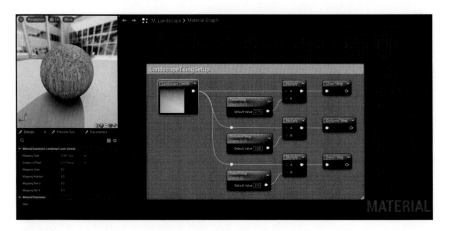

**FIGURE 5.23**   Landscape tiling setup.

This next section leverages our tiling setup and some of Unreal's Material Functions to break up repetition on Landscapes. There are a couple of different ways of doing this, we are going to use a Material Function called TextureVariation, you may also wish to try TextureBombing. Features like this are very much geared toward higher-end solutions, and on lower-end platforms, it's worth using Switch Parameters to disable costly features when required.

Let's get building!

1. Right Click in the Material Graph and search for *DistanceTiling*. This should call a direct link to our Named Reroute node.
2. Drag out from the **DistanceTiling** node and from the pop-up menu search for the *TextureVariation* node. It's possible to add in a lot of Parameters to this node to control its behavior, however, in this example, we are going to use it with the default properties.
3. Drag out of the **TextureVariation** node and search for the *Named Reroute Declaration* node, call this node *DstTilingUVVariation*. We will use this later with a bunch of textures.
4. Now we need to repeat the above but for CloseTiling. Move below in the Material Graph and Right Click, search for *CloseTiling*.
5. Drag out from the **CloseTiling** node and from the pop-up menu, search for a *TextureVariation* node.
6. Drag out of the **TextureVariation** node and search for the *Named Reroute Declaration* node, call this node *CloseTilingUVVariation*.
7. You can compare your work against Figure 5.24.

Now that we've built ways to adjust Tiling and then UV variation, we need to add some logic to select which UV Tiling is used. Unreal doesn't know how to UV map our textures against our Landscape, so we need to give it some way of understanding where the Camera is in our Game Worlds and then use this to blend between appropriate UVs. We are going to build a solution that works with and without RVT.

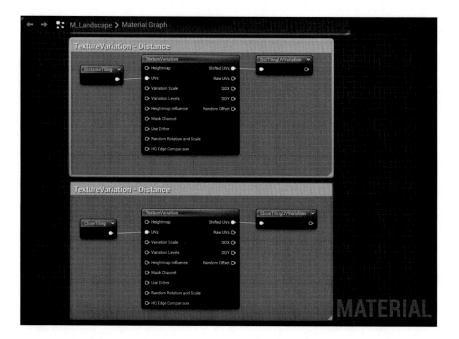

**FIGURE 5.24**   Texture variation UVs.

Let's get started!

1. Move below our **Texture Variation** nodes in the Material Graph.
2. Right Click in the Material Graph and search for *View Property*. Change the **View Property** value in the **Details** panel to *Virtual Texture Output Level*.
3. Drag out from the **Property** pin on the **Virtual Texture Output Level** and search for a *Power* node. Disconnect the **Virtual Texture Output Level** nodes connection from **Base** to **Exp**.
4. Next, create a **Scalar Parameter** node by holding down S and Left Clicking, label this node *RVT Power* using the **Details** panel. Finally, set its **Default Value** to *2* and connect it to the **Base** input on the **Power** node.
5. Create a **Multiply** node by holding M and Left Clicking in the Material Graph. Connect the Output of the **Power** node into the **A** input of the **Multiply** and set the **B** value to be *1000*.
6. Drag out from the **Multiply** node and search for an *Add* node from the pop-up menu.
7. Right click on the **B** input and select **Promote to Parameter**. Set the **Scalar Parameter** name to be *FadeStartingPoint* and set its **Default Value** to be *–10000*.
8. Next, drag out from the **Add** node and search for a *Divide* node from the pop-up menu.
9. Right click on the **B** input and select **Promote to Parameter**. Set the **Scalar Parameter** name to be *Fade Length* and set its **Default Value** to be *150000*.

10. Now drag out from the **Divide** node and search for the node *Virtual Texture Feature Switch* from the pop-up menu.
11. Make sure the **Divide** node is connected to **Yes** (it will default to **No**).
12. Drag backward from the **No** input on the **Virtual Texture Feature Switch** node and search for *Distance Blend* from the pop-up menu.
13. Right Click on both **Blend Range** and **Start Offset** inputs and select **Promote to Parameter**. For the **Blend Range** Scalar Parameter, label this as *FadeLength* and set its **Default Value** to be *150000*. For the **StartOffset** Parameter, label this as *FadeStartingPoint* and set its **Default Value** to be *150000*.
14. Lastly, drag out from the **VirtualTextureFeatureSwitch** node and search for the *Named Reroute Declaration* node, call this node *DistanceBlendUV*.
15. If all has gone well, you should have a result that looks similar to Figure 5.25.

We now have two ways to blend Distance-Based Tiling. When testing the Material in multiple levels, you may wish to use Material Instances as a way to leverage different distance blending numbers. Don't feel confined by the values, experiment with these and see what works for you.

We now need to update our four **MF_LandscapeLayer** Functions to support our tiling and variation feature set. You may need to make a bit of space vertically as we go through these amends, don't try to keep the graph the same as we'll be adding a lot of nodes.

Let's get started!

1. Move over to the **Mud MF_LandscapeLayer** section of the Graph.
2. Duplicate the **MudRoughnessMask** node and place the two nodes so they stack vertically.
3. Drag backward from the **UV** input of the top **MudRoughnessMask** node and search for *CloseTilingUVVariation* from the pop-up menu.
4. Drag backward from the **UV** input of the lower **MudRoughnessMask** node and search for *DstTilingUVVariation* from the pop-up menu.

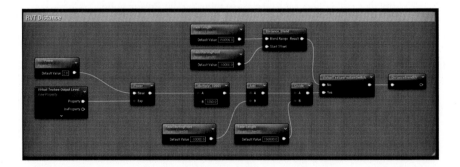

**FIGURE 5.25**   RVT distance blending.

5. Right Click in the Material Graph and search for *DistanceBlendUV*, leave this node just below the lower **DstTilingUVVariation** node for now. This should mean the three inputs are aligned.

6. Next, create a Linear Interpolate Node by holding L and Left Clicking in the **Material Graph**. Connect the top **MudRoughnessMask** node's Green Channel (**G** pin) into the **A** input of the **Lerp** node.

7. Connect the lower **MudRoughnessMask** node's Green Channel into the **B** input of the **Lerp** node.

8. Connect the **Distance Blend UV Output** into the **Alpha** input of the **Lerp** node.

9. Next, connect the output of the **Lerp** node into the **Roughness Mask** input of the **MF_LandscapeLayer** node.

10. You can review your work by looking at Figure 5.26.

You will need to follow the above approach for each Texture in your graph, we are effectively duplicating the total amount of textures and then using our new Distance Blend and Tiling to functions to drive everything.

To complete the updating process, you need to go through each Texture Input of the Material Functions and set up Linear Interpolation, as shown in Figure 5.26. There are some caveats to be aware of, which we'll now address.

- When updating Normal and Base Color Textures you must connect to the **Lerp** node by using the **RGB** pin and not the Green Channel (**G** pin).

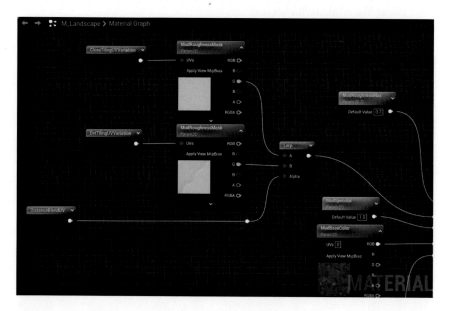

**FIGURE 5.26**   Updating material UVs.

- The **Detail Normal** node, requires only the input of the named reroute **DetailTiling**. You can find this node by Right Clicking in the Material Graph and searching for the **DetailTiling** node, and then connecting its output to any **DetailNormalTexture** (four in total).
- Keep your layout simple, Figure 5.27 shows a relatively tidy graph with reroute nodes added to ensure things don't overlap too much.
- This update will take a while to implement as there's a lot to move about. Make use of keyboard shortcuts like Q to align nodes horizontally and SHIFT+A to align nodes vertically, these should help you maintain the tidiness of the Material.

There's one feature we need to revisit before closing this chapter, and that's our Specular pass. We now have a mechanism to fade specularity over distance, this is helpful as we don't want our terrain to sparkle consistently for hundreds of meters. We are going to use our **DistanceBlend** node as a mask to help fade the Specularity across the landscape.

Let's get started.

1. Navigate over to our previously created specular nodes, which can be seen in Figure 5.14.
2. Disconnect the **B** input from the **Lerp** node.
3. Drag backward from the **B** input and from the menu search for a *Multiply* node.
4. Connect the **A** input of the **Multiply** node to the **Specular** output of the **BreakMaterialAttributes** node.

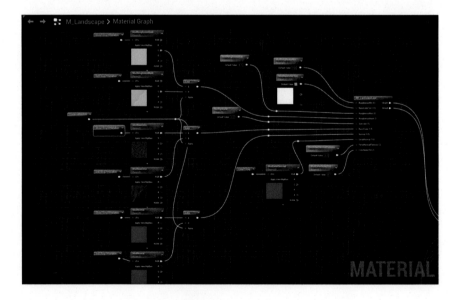

**FIGURE 5.27**   Reworking our material functions.

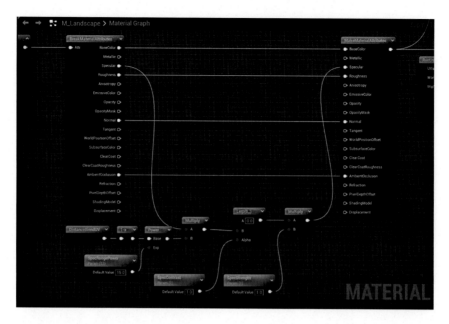

**FIGURE 5.28** Distance scaling specular.

5. Drag backward from the **B** input of the **Multiply** node and search for a *Power* node from the pop-up menu.

6. Drag backward from the **Base** input of the **Power** node and search for a *OneMinus* node from the pop-up menu.

7. Right Click on the **Power** node's **Exp** input and select to **Promote to Parameter**. Set the **Scalar Parameter** name to be *Spec Range Power* and set its **Default Value** to be *15*.

8. Lastly, drag back from the **One Minus** node's input and search for the *DistanceBlendUV* node from the pop-up menu.

9. You will now have the ability to fade specularity over distance, use Figure 5.28 to review your work.

To see exactly what is going on, try changing the Viewport from Lit Mode to the Buffer Specular channel. Figure 5.29 shows the example falloff as the further back the Landscape is. Remember to set the Viewport back to Lit Mode after you are done.

## Conclusion

We are now feature complete for the Landscape Material, for now… This Material affords many of the modern requirements for a Landscape except automated painting and foliage. We'll explore both of these features separately to help push our powers even further. If you'd like to see a rough overview of the Material, take a look at Figure 5.30. You can also take a look at our completed materials in the **Content Browser**, navigate to the **Completed | Master | Materials** folder.

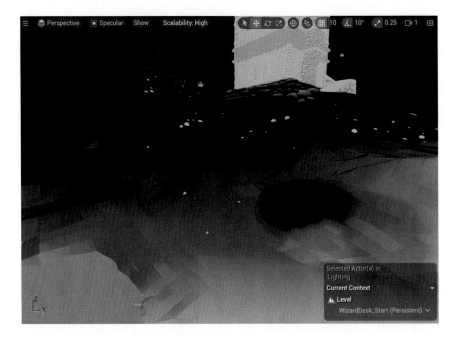

**FIGURE 5.29**  Specular buffer preview.

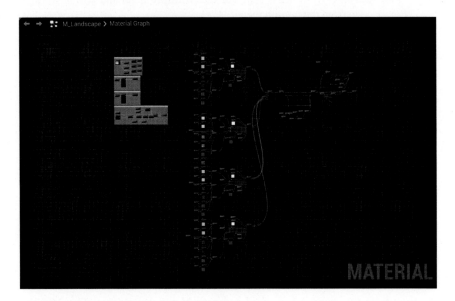

**FIGURE 5.30**  Landscape material graph overview.

In Chapter 6, we'll begin to explore how to use Unreals Foliage systems to help decorate our Landscapes. Before we carry on, let's review this chapter's quiz.

## Chapter 5  Quiz

Question 1: What does RVT stand for?

    a. Run Visual Targets.

    b. Random Vector Truths.

    c. Runtime Virtual Texturing.

    d. Random Variable Textures.

Question 2: What's the benefit of Named Reroute Nodes when making large Materials?

    a. Named Reroute nodes open up locked parts of the Material Editor.

    b. Named Reroute nodes help keep large graphs tidy by avoiding the placement of too many connection lines.

    c. Named Reroute nodes Make Material calculations run faster.

Question 3: What happens if we do not control specularity in our Landscape Materials?

    a. If our specular control is poor, our Landscape will look like concrete.

    b. If our specular control is poor, we can end up with a soft white sheen on our Landscapes.

    c. If our specular control is poor, our Landscapes do not build lighting.

Question 4: What is the benefit of using Material Functions in Landscape Materials.

    a. Landscape Materials often have repetitive structures, Material Functions help to keep these structures consistent across teams and save time.

    b. Material Functions Make Material run 4* faster.

    c. Material Functions Make Material Graphs look prettier.

### Answers

Question 1: c

Question 2: b

Question 3: b

Question 4: a

# 6

## Foliage

### Introduction to Unreal Foliage Tools

In this chapter, we are going to explore two ways of working with Foliage in Unreal. But what is Foliage?

Foliage inside of Unreal can be thought of as anything from small blades of grass to large trees, as World Builders, we are responsible for decorating our Landscapes with Foliage and we are fortunate to have a variety of systems at hand to make this process a joy inside of the Unreal Editor.

We will start with utilizing Unreal's Foliage Mode, much like the Landscape Mode we've used in previous chapters, this is a set of tools dedicated to one task. Foliage Mode features the ability to load in multiple meshes to help build up an artist's palette of foliage assets. Each asset has multiple properties to help you realize the exact look and art direction needed. Finally, the toolset allows us to paint directly in our world, where we want our Foliage Meshes to appear.

Foliage Mode is a very artistically driven toolset and shall form a good chunk of your world decoration pipeline on small-to-medium worlds, however, as you move onto larger worlds you may wish to utilize some forms of automatic foliage placement to do the heavy lifting.

For the second approach, we'll begin to venture into this area via Unreal's Procedural Foliage System. The Procedural System allows us to build up foliage assets with many properties that can be linked to Material Landscape Layers and many other World Properties.

Linking with Materials enables the Foliage System to automatically populate landscapes. Smart workflows like this can reduce the time needed for spawning many thousands of meshes, however, it should never fully replace manual decoration. Procedural art is a double-edged sword, while it can offer significant efficiencies in development time, used too frequently, your worlds may lack character or finesse. Our suggestion is to build up large chunks of your work with procedural features and then use artistic toolsets to refine and detail the most important areas of your worlds.

So, what should we be aware of before starting to decorate our worlds?

1. **Pivots** – To place foliage assets easily, it's good to have pivots placed centrally but underneath your foliage asset. Try to get into the headspace of thinking you are gluing an asset onto a surface.
2. **Alpha Cards/Textures** – These can be a significant cause of Overdraw and cause a drop in frame rate in a game. Try to maximize your UV usage of any Alpha texture to reduce any unnecessary Overdraw.

DOI: 10.1201/9781032663883-6

3. **Shadows** – It's worth evaluating what shadow-casting options your game has and whether they are required for your art style. Casting shadows across many thousands of foliage meshes can be very expensive, at the very least, it's worth exploring if you should disable shadow casting at a certain distance.

4. **Face Normals** – These can dramatically affect the look of your foliage in-game. It's worth speaking with 3D artists should your foliage look strange or poor from the very start. Meshes like bushes often require normal baking from spheres or proxy geometry to enable a good visual result, whereas grass assets might require Face Normals pointing upward to avoid incorrect shading.

5. **Nanite** – Foliage assets are a tricky problem for Nanite due to most construction workflows currently utilizing alpha cards. Epic's own approach has recently shifted to create trees and foliage assets in several stages using meshes and not alpha cards.

With the key considerations understood, we can start working with Foliage.

## Creating Our First Foliage Asset

To begin working with Foliage, we first need to swap to Foliage Mode. The specific mode has lots of tools and options for us to work with. It operates, just like the Selection and Landscape Modes we have used so far, with many parameters and details to customize.

The overall process we will follow is to open Foliage Mode and then import the Meshes we wish to paint on a Landscape. When the meshes have been imported we will go through the settings which control a variety of features such as density, scale, angle and even lighting. Once a Foliage Asset has been set up we can then paint and erase the Foliage Asset in the world using a Foliage Brush.

Figure 6.1 shows the Foliage Mode UI. Typically, we work bottom upward, you need to find static meshes in the Content Browser and then drag and drop them onto the Foliage UI where it says **Drop Foliage Here**. This then creates a Foliage Asset for us to manipulate and use within our world.

As you begin to set up and customize a variety of Foliage Assets, you will see thumbnails of the Foliage appear at the bottom of the Foliage Mode UI. The thumbnails themselves are quite useful, not just to help you recognize what plant or asset you are manipulating, but also because the UI shows how many instances of the asset are present in the level, and also gives you the ability to turn the Foliage Asset on and off. The ability to turn on and off assets will not remove the Foliage from the Level, but it will prevent you from painting or adding further instances when you don't want to, it may not be evident to begin with, but it's quite easy to set up five assets and paint them all at the same time however we suggest that you work with one asset at a time for the most part. Start with painting in the most common mesh before working through less and less common types until you reach what we would suggest is the hero/focal point foliage. This is where we paint very specific types that are likely to gather the player/viewers attention.

Let's get started!!

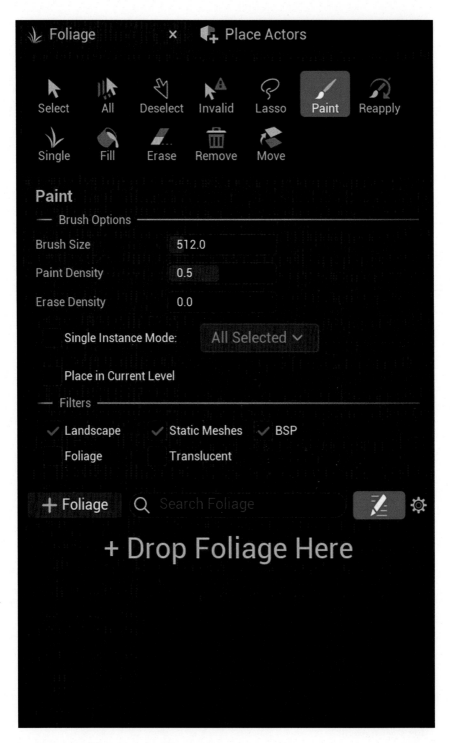

**FIGURE 6.1** Foliage mode UI overview.

## Painting Foliage Assets

To begin, open a Level that contains a Landscape Actor and a Landscape Material. These can be your own creations or you could open the WizardDesk_Start level, which is available in the Maps folder in the Content Browser. When everything is open, you can get started:

1. Swap to *Foliage Mode* using the mode drop down or by pressing SHIFT + 3.
2. Using the **Content Browser,** navigate to the **Content | Meshes** folder and search for *Grass.*
3. Drag and Drop the **GrassMediumClump1** static mesh onto the Foliage Mode UI where it says **Drop Foliage Here.**
4. You will then be prompted to save a Foliage asset. There are already a couple of these assets in the project, we suggest that you don't overwrite them and make your own *FoliageAssets* folder inside the **Meshes** directory by Right Clicking on the **Meshes** folder and selecting **New Folder** from the menu. You can then label your Foliage Asset *GrassMediumClump1_FoliageType.*
5. When the Foliage Asset is complete, your UI should match with that of Figure 6.2.
6. You can test Foliage Painting at this point, holding Left Mouse will add foliage meshes to the world and holding CTRL + SHIFT + Left Mouse will erase meshes.

At this point, you may notice some issues, for example, very noisy/distracting shadows, and the grass is quite large. We can adjust both of these very easily within the Foliage Mode UI, however if the scale at this point is ever ridiculous or your pivot point is in the wrong place, you may wish to improve these in a modeling package such as 3ds Max, Maya and/or Blender.

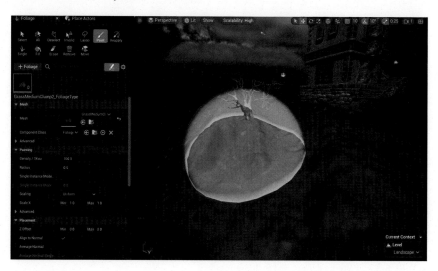

**FIGURE 6.2** Painting grass.

We'll now adjust some settings to improve our painting. An important thing to note is that updated changes only apply to meshes that are painted/created after settings have been tweaked. I find it easier to do little test paints to start with to get my settings exactly right and then paint big areas. Try to avoid spending a long time painting and then having to erase lots of work because settings aren't perfected. With that said, let's now improve our density and scale:

1. Make sure your Foliage Asset is enabled, when you hover over it in the **Foliage Mode** preview you'll see a tickbox, ensure it is on.

2. Next, Scroll Down to the **Painting Options**. Increasing the **Density** options will spawn more Foliage meshes. Increasing the **Radius** will increase the gap between meshes. This can be helpful if you want to place trees or larger items that aren't directly on top of one another. For now, though, set **Density** to *2000* and leave the **Radius** set to *0*. This will spawn a lot more grass.

3. Next, look for the **Scale X** setting, by default, the Scale on a Foliage Asset is uniform, so we only adjust one axis to affect all three. We are provided with the options to have a **Max** and **Min** value. One is a bit high so try a value of *0.5* for both and paint some new Foliage in the world and see how it changes.

4. You may check your settings against Figure 6.3.

5. Next, scroll a bit further to **Instance Settings**. Here, we can adjust how Foliage Meshes are lit. There are many options to dive into.

6. Disable **Cast Dynamic**, **Contact** and **Static Shadows**.

7. Check Figure 6.4 for a comparison of settings. It's not always necessary to disable foliage shadows but some games may require it, particularly if they run on lower end platforms.

**FIGURE 6.3**   Changing density and scale settings.

**FIGURE 6.4** Customizing shadows.

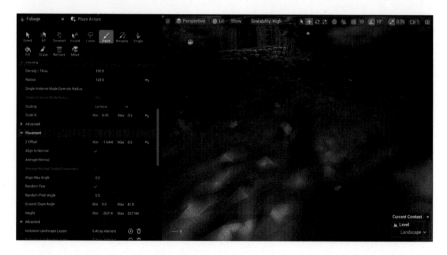

**FIGURE 6.5** Scale variety for painting rocks.

Now you've seen how to add Meshes and change some basic properties, try adding further static meshes from the Content Browser to the Foliage Mode. Each new Foliage Mesh will require you to save a Foliage asset, keep your naming conventions and locations consistent to help other artists.

Another asset that's worth trying is a rock or a pebble, they tend to have a larger variety in shape and sizes which is fun to try and customize. In Figure 6.5, a rock has been set up that has a wide range in Scale X to create a range of rocks from large rocks down to very small pebbles. In addition, you'll see that the Z Offset has been customized. This option is great when you need to sink a mesh into the ground, this can be very helpful for rocks and trees as they can have quite uneven bases.

**FIGURE 6.6**    Painting settings.

Another important option to explore is Align to Normal, this option will place a Foliage mesh based on the normal of the Landscape surface underneath. This may seem harmless, but if you want to place trees/flowers that grow upright toward the sun, be sure to disable Align to Normal before you start painting. You should spot the mistake straight away as your forests will look very wonky if this property is not correct.

It's worth noting there are many painting options for placing foliage. Figure 6.6 showcases some of the options you have in addition to painting and erasing foliage. You may, for example, find it easier to lasso and remove sections of foliage in larger areas rather than trying to manually erase. The filters' options are also very useful and allow you to target specific actors like Landscapes and avoid painting on meshes or accidental areas. It's certainly worth getting the brush size and filter setup early on in your painting adventures.

## Setting Up Our Static Mesh Foliage

We are now going to explore creating some procedural foliage. The idea here is that we won't have to paint or place our foliage in the level. We'll be able to use Unreal to do the creation work based on some rules and properties we develop.

In order for us to work on this section, we need to enable some tools which are deactivated by default.

1. Head over to the top menu and select **Edit | Editor Settings**, you should now see a new pop-up menu.

2. Use the search box and type *Procedural*, you should now have the option to enable a checkbox labeled **Procedural Foliage**. This will now update the Editor UI to allow us to create a few more assets and work with the Procedural Spawner.

3. You can review the checkbox in Figure 6.7, note this is different from enabling an Engine Plugin and should not require you to restart the Editor.

With the Procedural Foliage setting activated, we are ready to begin so let's get creating!

1. Navigate to the **Content | Landscape** folder in the **Content Browser**.

2. Right Click and select **Foliage | Static Mesh Foliage** from the pop-up menu. Label this new asset *GrassMedium_InstancedStaticMeshFoliage*.

3. Right click against and select **Foliage | Procedural Foliage Spawner** from the pop-up menu. Label this new asset *GrassProceduralFoliageSpawner*.

4. Figures 6.8 and 6.9 show the location of these new assets, if your Editor doesn't have the Procedural Foliage tickbox enabled, then these options will not be present. Please revisit the earlier section if this is the case.

**FIGURE 6.7**  Enabling the procedural foliage tools.

**FIGURE 6.8**  Creating a static mesh foliage asset.

**FIGURE 6.9** Creating a procedural foliage spawner.

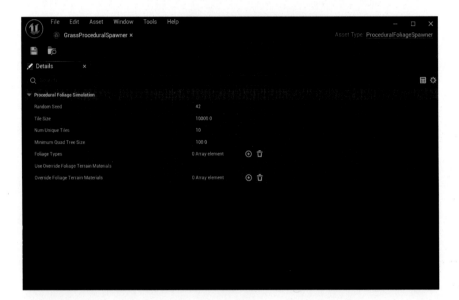

**FIGURE 6.10** Exploring the procedural foliage spawner properties.

## Creating Our Procedural Foliage Spawner

Now that we have our assets in place, let's explore what they do and then try them out. To start with, we are going to work with GrassProceduralFoliageSpawner. We will use this asset as a volumetric shape. Unreal will try to calculate the creation of Foliage within a box volume. To do this, we configure Brush settings, set what actors are considered in the logic and then resimulate our logic. Before we can use the Spawner in a level, we have to set some initial properties.

1. Double Click on the **GrassProceduralFoliageSpawner** asset in the **Content Browser**. The options will look the same as Figure 6.10.
2. Next, click the + button next to **Foliage Types**.
3. Then we need to set the **Foliage Type** to *GrassMedium_InstancedStatic MeshFoliage*.

4. We can populate this array with as many Foliage assets as we want, rocks, trees, flowers, etc., however, the more complicated we make this array, the longer it will take for the Spawner to run.

We are now going to set up our GrassMedium_InstancedStaticMeshFoliage asset. Many of the things we are going to do will be familiar to the Foliage Mode options. To get started, you need to find the asset in the Content Browser and double click it to begin, let's explore:

1. First, set the **Mesh Property** to *Meshes/GrassMediumClump1*.
2. Next, set the **Z Placement Min** and **Max** to *0.2*, which lifts the model upward slightly.
3. Scroll Down the options and find the **Ground Slope Angle** property, set the **Min** to be *0* and the **Max** to be *25*. This means that any slopes above 25 degrees or below 0 will be ignored.
4. Now search for the property **Inclusion Landscape Layers**, use the + button to add an entry to the array. Set **Index [0]** to be *Grass*. This will mean that our Foliage will only be drawn on Landscape layers that have been defined as Grass. You can review your progress so far by comparing against Figure 6.11.
5. Scroll down to the **Collision** settings. Lower the **Collision Radius** and **Shade Radius** to *10*, this allows the Grass planes to spawn much closer together.

**FIGURE 6.11**    Setting up foliage static mesh placement and basic properties.

6. Under the **Clustering** options, raise the **Initial Seed Density** to *15*. This will increase the possibility of spawning Grass. Do not set this too high, as it can cause crashes.

7. Set the **Average Spread Distance** to *12* and **Spread Variance** to *65*.

8. You can compare your progress here against Figure 6.12.

9. Locate the **Growth** properties. Set **Can Grow in Shade** to *True*.

10. Set **Spawns in Shade** to *True*.

11. Set the **Max Initial Age** to *10*.

12. Set the **Procedural Scale Min** and **Max** to *0.2*, these values are worth experimenting with to try and find out the correct sizing of your foliage.

13. Under the **Instance** settings, disable **Cast Shadow**.

14. You can now save the asset and compare the values against those in Figure 6.13.

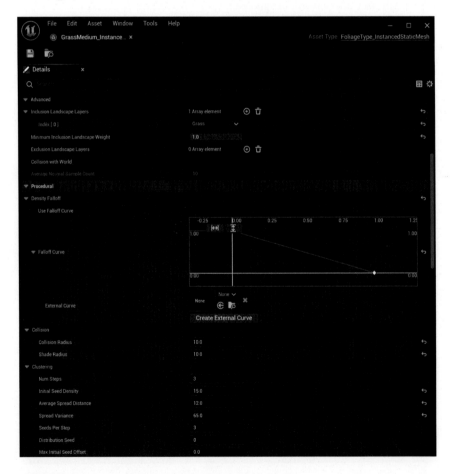

**FIGURE 6.12**    Setting up foliage static mesh procedural properties.

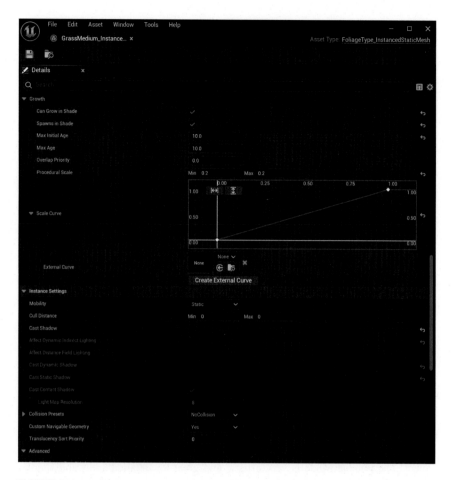

**FIGURE 6.13** Setting up foliage static mesh growth and instances properties.

To test our Procedural Spawner, you need to locate the GrassProceduralFoliageSpawner and drag and drop the asset into the Editor Viewport. This will create a Level Actor for you.

From here, use the actors Brush settings to set the scale, configure any filters/options, and click Resimulate. The process will then spawn the Foliage Meshes as an Instanced Foliage Actor. Figure 6.14 shows this actor in action, note that to test this, I placed the Brush Volume over part of the landscape where I had painted grass. Without the Grass done, this will result in no Foliage Meshes appearing, also note that the Foliage Meshes do not cover the entirety of the painted grass on the landscape, this is because the slope is too high!

Be careful when utilizing the Spawner Actors, it's very easy to crash the engine by over complicating the logic or by making the actor too big. In some cases, it's worth getting a drink or doing something else for a short time while Unreal works.

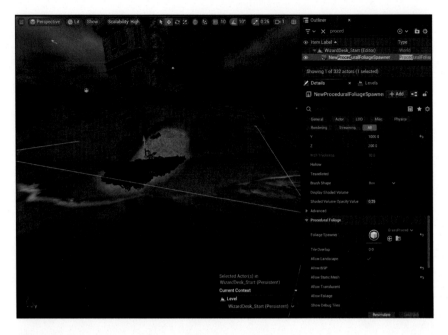

**FIGURE 6.14**   In editor example GrassProceduralFoliageSpawner.

## Conclusion

We've now explored placing Foliage quickly with painting-style tools and procedural volumes. Both are great options and you'll often choose to use them both on the same project. The Foliage Mode is very artistic and great for detailed areas and smaller projects. The Procedural Spawner is great for very fast creation but it can only be as good as the rules that are fed into the system.

Fortunately, with the advances of other parts of Unreal Engine such as the Procedural Content Graph (PCG), it's possible to build even more complex rules for Foliage creation. We suggest trying the Procedural Foliage Tools out first in this chapter and then delving into PCG when you need to create something more complex.

Another option for you to review is Unreal's Grass System. In comparison to the systems, we've explored here, Grass Assets will automatically spawn if they are set up in the Material Editor. The asset is simple to use and creates Meshes linked to Landscape Layer Blends. However, it does have a drawback, which is that you cannot exceed the density (overall amount of grass) without C++ at the time of writing. So if your Landscape is scaled in a particular way or is too large, the system falls down a little. Still, it's very powerful and worth exploring should you wish to try out another engine toolset.

In Chapter 7, we'll begin to explore Unreal's Water Plugins to help bring further life to our worlds. But first, a short quiz!

## Chapter 6 Quiz

Question 1: What is the way we should add Static Meshes to Foliage Mode?

    a. Drag and Drop them from the Content Browser.

    b. Import FBX.

    c. Create a Foliage Collection.

Question 2: What property should we ensure is disabled when placing Trees?

    a. Align to Normal.

    b. Align to Landscape.

    c. Align to Up.

    d. DotNormalZ.

Question 3: What do we need to enable to use the Procedural Foliage Toolset?

    a. We need to enable the Tree Plugin in the FAB Marketplace.

    b. We need to enable the Procedural Foliage Checkbox in the Editor Settings.

    c. We need to use the Seed Blueprint to Grow Trees.

Question 4: Why do we need to be cautious when using the Procedural Foliage Spawner Actors?

    a. We need to configure every option or they will not operate.

    b. The Actors work best when placing tiny trees.

    c. If we make them too large and the ruleset is too complex, it's easily possible to make Unreal Hang or Crash.

## Answers

Question 1: a

Question 2: a

Question 3: b

Question 4: c

# 7

## Water

## Introduction to Unreal Water Tools

Unreal's Water Plugins are a collection of spline-based editor tools that allows us to create bodies of water such as Rivers, Lakes and Oceans. The toolset supports features such as Wave Rendering, Physics, Fluid Simulation and Interaction with gameplay. To begin working with the toolset, we need to enable a couple of plugins. In this chapter, we'll add a few of those tools to a demo level and slowly build up a water system.

> ### IMPORTANT NOTE
>
> At the time of writing, the Water Tools are still experimental which means the information we discuss will change, features will be updated and removed, and you may find some pretty glorious bugs. However, even in the experimental state, these tools are really powerful and fun to use, we are certain you are going to enjoy them! If you find that many of the experimental features of the Water System have been updated, install Unreal 5.3.2 and you'll be able to enjoy this Chapter. Keep an eye on Epic's documentation to see the latest updates!

## Enabling the Water Plugins

To get started with the Water System, open up the project and open the level Water_ Start ready for using the tools.

1. First, we need to enable the Water Systems, to do this navigate to **Edit | Plugins** and then search in the Plugin Dialogue box for *Water*. You will see both **Water** and **Water Extras**.
2. Select both of these Plugins, as shown in Figure 7.1.

**FIGURE 7.1** Water plugins.

DOI: 10.1201/9781032663883-7

You will then be asked to restart the Editor, this only happens the first time you enable the Plugins, however you will have to do this each time you enable the Water System in an Unreal Project.

## Water Body Actors

We can now access several Water Actors with the plugin enabled. To start this section, you need to:

1. In the **Content Browser**, navigate to the folder **Content | Maps** and open the **Landscape_WaterTools_Start** level.
2. Navigate to the **Place Actors** Menu and type *Water*.
3. You should now see a list of Actors, as shown in Figure 7.2.

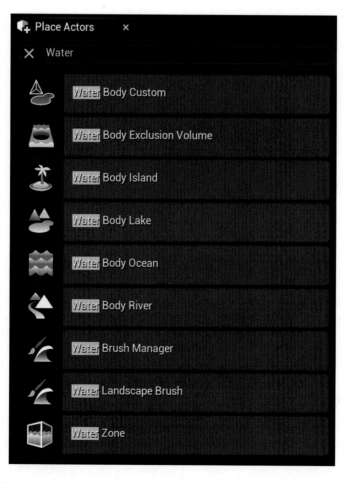

**FIGURE 7.2** Placeable water actors.

**FIGURE 7.3** Starting landscape.

**FIGURE 7.4** Enable edit layers.

The actors we'll explore first are called Water Bodies which comprises Oceans, Lakes and Rivers. Many of these actors operate through spline manipulation that affects their visual appearance and function.

To begin with, your scene should look like the example shown in Figure 7.3.

When a Water Body is added to the world, it will automatically adjust existing Landscape Terrain. In order for this to function, your Landscape must have "Enable Edit Layers" set to True. This setting can be toggled upon creation of a terrain in the Landscape Mode or in the Details Panel for existing Landscapes. This setting is shown in Figure 7.4.

## Setting Up Water Body Ocean Actors

Before we begin, It's important to note that many of the Water System Bodies leverage detailed tessellated meshes that increase a level's performance cost. To mitigate this, you will need to leverage the Far Distance parameters in the Waterzone Actors. Here, we can swap in more simplistic materials at a specified distance to help lower rendering costs. Each game or level will have different performance options, values like Far

Distance Mesh Extent will need to be set per project, by default, it's set to 400000 Unreal Units. Regardless of project, the goal of this parameter is to ensure that the Ocean fills any gaps between itself and the horizon line.

1. Drag a **Water Body Ocean Actor** from the **Place Actor** menu into the current Level. Here, we can see a closed spline loop helps to create a shoreline/island, and the Ocean Water body then extends outward.
2. We can manipulate the size and shape of the shoreline by adjusting a **Water Body Ocean** Actor's **Spline Component**. To do this, navigate to the **Details Panel** and select the **Spline Component** from the list.
3. Alter the size of the shore by selecting the white vertex points on the spline in the viewport and then use Unreal's transform tools to manipulate the shoreline.

The default Water Body Ocean Actor has a Falloff set to angle, this erodes at the sides of the Landscape and turns the level into an island. For example, in Figure 7.5, we can see that the perimeter of the Landscape has been eroded away. Sometimes we might want this, particularly if we are trying to create something like a Tropical island erupting out of the ocean.

Let's say we want to be able to see the Ocean in the background from certain vantage points of the level, but we don't want the Ocean to erode the Landscape so severely. Let's look at how we can achieve a less dramatic erosion:

1. In the **Details** panel, find the **Falloff Mode** parameter in the **Water Heightmap Settings** section. Change it to *Width*.
2. Then lower the **Falloff Width** to *64.0* and the **Edge Offset** to *16.0* so that the Ocean doesn't erode the Landscape so aggressively. Figure 7.6 shows this result.

Another setting which has a significant impact in how the actor affects our Landscape is the Blend Mode parameter, let's try experimenting with one of the options:

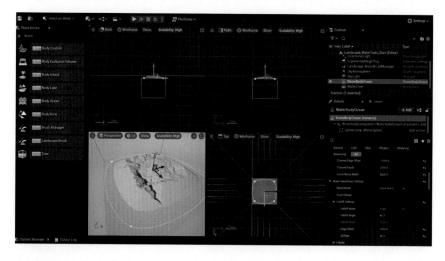

**FIGURE 7.5** Previewing the water body ocean actor angle fall off.

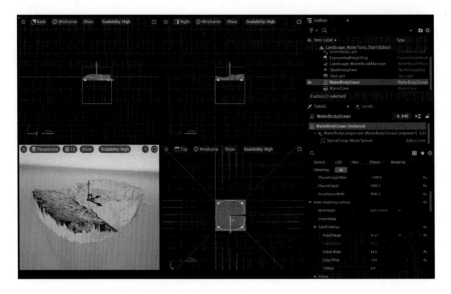

**FIGURE 7.6**   Water body ocean width falloff.

1. Set the **Blend Mode** to *Max*.
2. Move the **Water Body Ocean** Actor downwards in the level, you'll notice that it cuts away at the Landscape in a different manner.
3. Selecting the **Spline Component**, scale down the size of the shape using the Transform tools, with this, you can easily produce an inland sea, instead of an island.

We can have even further control by modifying the shape of the spline component by adjusting the spline points and their tangents, this is helpful as it affords us the opportunity to make a much more complex shape:

1. Click on one of the spline points, this will reveal its spline handles, which control the tangents in and out of each spline point.
2. Click and drag one of the handles around the point and then toward and away, explore how this modifies the shape of the spline and the resulting body of water.
3. The **Water Body Ocean** Actor has four spline points upon creation, we can modify the shape further by adding more spline points. Add an additional point by selecting one of the existing points, holding down ALT and Left Click dragging away from the point.

When modifying curves, try to avoid adding too many as controlling the shoreline with 100's of points can become time consuming and tricky. Try to combine the use of additional points and the tangent handles to achieve your desired shape. Figure 7.7 shows how the Ocean's shore can become more detailed with only a couple of extra points, with Figure 7.8 showcasing a larger view of the Landscape itself.

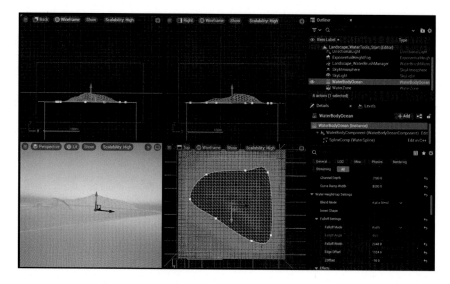

**FIGURE 7.7**   Adding more spline points.

**FIGURE 7.8**   Previewing the landscape with additional falloff.

**FIGURE 7.9**   Disabling affects landscape.

So far, we've explored how to use the Water Body Ocean Actor to produce bodies of water and manipulate the shape of the Landscape. For your project, you might prefer for the Ocean to not affect the Landscape Actor at all. Perhaps you want some waves in the distance of a Level that you can see from certain vantage points. This is certainly possible; Figure 7.9 shows this result with the parameter Affects Landscape disabled. We can still shape and customize the Water Body but its shape and layout will not alter the Landscape Actor. If you want to try this out:

1. Add a new **Water Body Ocean Actor** from the **Place Actors** menu.
2. In the **Details** panel, disable **Affects Landscape.**
3. Adjust the size of the Water Body Ocean Actor as required.

## Water Body River Actors

With an Ocean setup in the background, we can now start to explore the other Water Body Actors. The next Water Body Actor we're going to explore is the Water Body River Actor, as the name suggests, this actor is used to produce rivers in our levels and landscapes.

1. Before we begin, re-enable **Affects Landscape** on the **Water Body Ocean** Actor.
2. First, Drag a **Water Body River Actor** from the **Place Actors** menu, drop it somewhere near the shoreline. You should experience something similar to Figure 7.10, which shows a Water Body River actor has been placed near the Landscape edge. The Actor connects quite nicely to the sea but ends somewhat abruptly in the Landscape itself.
3. The River Actor works in a similar way to the ocean with a spline component; however, it's primarily designed to be a Line/Curve of Spline points

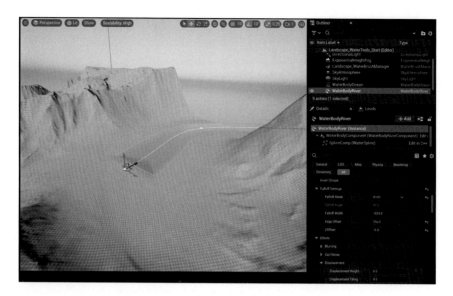

**FIGURE 7.10** Water body river.

dragged across a river's length. Extend the spline by adding additional spline points by selecting the last point on the spline, holding down ALT and dragging with the Left Mouse Button.

4. Repeat the process to join your shoreline with the inland **Water Body Ocean** Actor from earlier.

As additional spline points are created, the Landscape will deform to cater to the river's path. You'll also see a mesh plane with a water material applied weaving its way through the Landscape. One of the issues with the River Tool is that, by default, it has a consistent thickness like a crayon/felt pen. Let's explore how we can fix this by modifying the river's thickness.

1. Right Click on any spline point and from the pop-up menu select **Visualize River Width**.
2. You should now see two new handles appear that match up with the Rivers width, as shown in Figure 7.11.
3. These handles are very simple to use, select the points and then move the handles, this will adjust the width of the river.

It's worth adding several spline points to shape Rivers. Starting from an elevated source, your river should weave as it flows downward through your Landscape. As the river approaches, the sea we'd expect it to widen, whereas near the source, the river will often be at its narrowest.

Figure 7.12 shows an example of the River actor widening as it reaches the valley floor and connects to the sea. This has been achieved by adjusting some of the parameters, let's experiment with these.

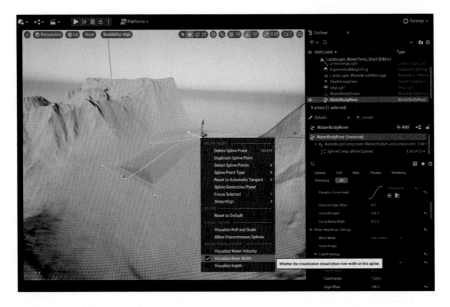

**FIGURE 7.11**    Visualizing river widths.

**FIGURE 7.12**    Growing river width from source to sea connection.

1. In the **Details** panel, locate **Falloff Mode** and set it to *Width*. This generally gives a better visual result as it will create a river bank.
2. Adjust the **Falloff Width** and **Edge Offset** parameters to see what effect they have on your landscape. Higher values will give you more space to pass around the river forming the river bank.

**FIGURE 7.13** Reducing falloff and edge offset.

3. Lower values will provide a much sharper transition similar to the one shown in Figure 7.13. Whilst this sort of result does occur naturally in the real world in hard rock areas, it can look a little strange if too severe, so be careful.

Ensure when creating rivers that you are utilizing reference to inform the plotting of a rivers course and major features. Feel free to explore the river tools and see how the different values may affect the Landscape.

## Setting Up Water Body Lake Actors

Water Body Lake Actors work much the same as Rivers and Ocean actors. However, they afford you the opportunity of placing a body of water in the middle of a Landscape and are a more purposeful option than using the Ocean in land, similar to what we did earlier. So let's replace that.

1. Delete the existing inland **Water Body Ocean** Actor if you still have it in your level.
2. Add a **Water Body Lake Actor** to the world from the **Place Actors** menu.
3. The default shape is triangular/3-point spline. This can be customized in the same manner as the other Water Actors. Select one of the points, hold ALT, Click and Drag existing spline points to add a few more.
4. In the **Details** panel, change the **Falloff Mode** to *Width*. Feel free to explore the other settings to control the effect the spline has on the Landscape.

Figure 7.14 shows default Water Body Lake Actor drag and dropped into the Level.

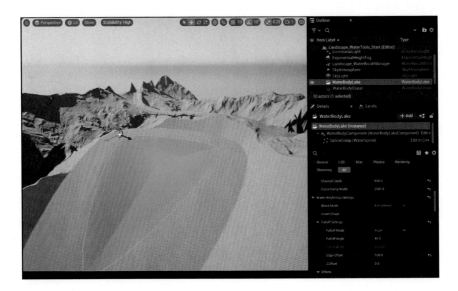

**FIGURE 7.14**　Water body lake.

**FIGURE 7.15**　Water body lake width falloff.

Much like the other two Water Body Actors, the Lake Actor looks better when the Falloff Mode is set to width, as shown in Figure 7.15. Again as per River and Ocean Actors, be mindful not give yourself enough of a falloff between the water and beach areas.

## Setting Up Extra River Actors

Your worlds can have multiple of the same Water Body Actors, if your Landscape is very large, it may make sense to be plotting a couple of rivers or lakes. In Figure 7.16, another Water Body River Actor connects our Main River to the Lake. The idea here was to create a river to feed the lake, albeit a much smaller and thinner river.

Try placing another river in your level and plot a course you're happy with. After placing a second river and adding additional spline points to connect the new River to the other River and Lake, you may find that the visual result leaves a bit to be desired, similar to the example shown in Figure 7.17. Even after tweaking Falloff or exploring

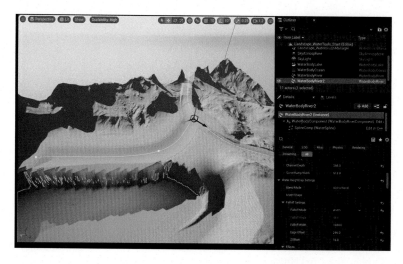

**FIGURE 7.16** Connecting water bodies, adding another water body river.

**FIGURE 7.17** Customizing water body river width and falloff.

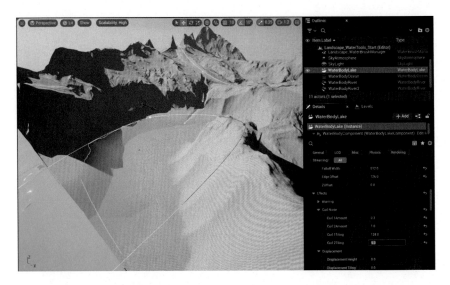

**FIGURE 7.18**    Adding curl noise to the water body lake actor.

smoothing options, the Landscape can look a bit too angular or pixelated, next we will explore an approach to improve the situation.

## Experimenting with Curl Noise

To improve the overall visual appearance of the Water Bodies, we can add noise:

1. Expand the **Curl Noise** properties, these give us the ability to add in two lots of noise.
2. Adjust the **Curl 1Amount** and **Curl 2Amount** variables to explore their effects on the result.
3. Likewise, adjust the **Curl 1Tiling** and **Curl 2Tiling** variables to see what effect they have.

Figures 7.18 and 7.19 show the results of Curl Noise applied to Lakes and Rivers at high tiling and low amounts. Be careful when adjusting the Amounts though, a value close to 1 can be very strong and have a very stylized/dramatic result. With the Tiling values, it can be helpful to have one of the values set high and the other low to add two very different types of noise.

## Further Customization

Figure 7.20 shows the visual result of four Water Body Actors dropped and a few property adjustments. The Water System is incredibly powerful and allows you to build interesting looking results very quickly. What's nice about these systems is that they all come with functioning materials and Landscape connections letting our choices impact other Unreal systems with ease.

**FIGURE 7.19** Adding curl noise to the water body river actors.

**FIGURE 7.20** Previewing all the water bodies.

### Customizing Water Materials

If you would like to further customize the appearance of the Water, for example, its color, speed, roughness, etc., search each WaterBody Actor for its Water Material. If you want to adjust properties, make a copy or an Instance of the applied Material, otherwise your changes will affect every other Unreal Engine project that utilizes water on your PC as these materials are in the Engine Content, not your Project Files.

Each Water Body comes with several Material Options, clicking on the Folder Icon with the spyglass will take you to the Original Material so that you can make a copy. We recommend storing any copies in the **Contents | Materials** folder. Once you've made duplicates you can apply them to your Water Body Actors and edit properties. Figure 7.21 shows the adjustment of the Absorption property which starts to darken the water and change its appearance away from the very clean tropical island default color.

### Customizing Waves

We can further art direct our Ocean by creating our own Water Waves Asset to control how the waves behave on our Water Body Actors.

1. To do this, **Right Click** inside the **Content folder** and create a New Folder Called *Water*.
2. Inside the **Water** folder, Right Click and create a **Water | Water Waves**.
3. You can name this asset however you wish. Once named, double click the asset to open the **Waves Editor**.
4. Inside the editor, we can customize many properties of our **Gestner Water Waves** asset. Using the **Details** panel, we can set many parameters ranging from **Num Waves**, which controls the number of waves to the overall amplitude of the waves, which is controlled by **Min Amplitude**, **Max Amplitude** and **Amplitude Falloff**.

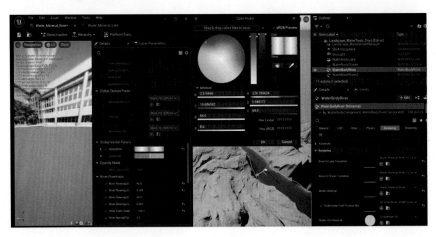

**FIGURE 7.21**   Adjusting water color.

**FIGURE 7.22** Wave editor preview.

5. When using this menu, do keep an eye on the **Waves Source Menu**, it can become collapsed and look like there are no properties to manipulate, so we suggest fully expanding this setting when the **Waves Editor** is open as shown in Figure 7.22.

6. When you are happy with your Waves appear, hit Save and close the Waves Editor.

7. Next, select the **WaterBodyOcean** Actor, and search for the *Water Wave Asset* property using the **Details** panel.

You should now see your waves update in the Viewport. Using this workflow, it's very easy to create your own calm sea or stormy ocean. For greater control, we suggest using two monitors, one to preview the Waves Editor and one to Preview the Levels Ocean, this saves the back and forth and closing of editors as you make changes.

## Conclusion

The Water Body system provides us with easy-to-use actors that have a similar workflow. This enables you to make sound workflow decisions for your Landscapes Water. One of the important factors that impacted almost all of the items discussed in this chapter is Falloff. The default Water Tool systems Falloff Mode is Angle which is quite severe for a Landscape that already has a height map/detailed appearance. You'll certainly need to spend plenty of time experimenting with spline points and falloff to get the look of your Rivers and Water Actors sorted.

After working on larger falloff shapes, it's worth then experimenting with noise to help breakup the perfect angles and lines that the tools may create. Try not to use too high values here as the results can end up very exaggerated.

In addition to what we've looked at in this chapter, you may also wish to experiment with the channel depth of the Water Bodies and also the Displacement textures to add further detail to the Landscape as the water cuts through the Landscape.

In Chapter 8, we'll explore how we can utilize Unreal's Landmass system to add even more detail to our Landscapes.

But first let's tackle this Chapters Quiz.

## Chapter 7  Quiz

Question 1: What is the first step we must follow to use the Water Tools in Unreal?

    a. We need to be in the Water Tool mode.

    b. We have to enable 2 plugins, Water and Water Extra.

    c. We need to make sure our Landscape has the CanBeWet Boolean checked.

Question 2: What is the main way of adjusting the shape of a Water Actor?

    a. We manipulate polygon vertices.

    b. We manipulate NURBS surfaces.

    c. We control spline points.

Question 3: What are the 4 main Water Body Types?

    a. Oceans, Rivers, Lakes and Islands.

    b. Oceans, Rivers, Puddles and Ponds.

    c. Rivers, Lakes, Streams and Ponds.

Question 4: What settings should we control to help blend a Water Body Actor with a Landscape?

    a. We can manually sculpt around the Water Body Actor using the Default Landscape Sculpting tools.

    b. In Shore Settings, we can set a shore distance that blends the Water Body with the Landscape.

    c. In Falloff Settings, we can control how a Water Body blends by Angle or Width along with many other parameters to help create a natural transition.

## Answers

Question 1: b

Question 2: c

Question 3: a

Question 4: c

# 8

## Landmass Tools

### Introduction to Landscape Materials

Unreal's basic Landscape sculpting tools are destructive, each user action destroys the record of the previous action. This is not always a bad thing, however, for artistic creativity, it's really nice to have the option to work non-destructively where possible. The reason for this is that it allows us to tweak and make changes easily, for example, you might sculpt a really nice lake bed but become dissatisfied with the background cliffs or rolling dunes. In a destructive setting, this may mean we have to alter both areas or start again to improve one section.

With the above in mind, it is worth exploring how we can work nondestructively in Unreal. Epic has created a great plugin called Landmass. The Landmass plugin allows us to create nondestructive Landscape Blueprint Brushes, which leave us with infinitely tweakable settings. To access the plugin in older versions of Unreal, you will need to activate Landmass by using the Edit | Plugins menu, with Unreal 5.3, the tools are enabled by default.

With the toolset enabled, it integrates with the existing Unreal Landscape Sculpting tools. Importantly when making a Landscape you must "Enable Edit Layers" for the Landmass Blueprint Brushes to work. This fortunately is enabled by default when you create a New Landscape in Unreal, however, should you accidently disable this, you can re-enable it on a Landscape actor by searching for the parameter in the Details panel. Note that enabling Edit Layers via the Details Panel will empty the undo/redo buffer.

Once you have a Landscape Actor in your level with Enable Edit Layers enabled, you can begin to explore the power of Landmass. As mentioned previously, its purpose is to provide us with a nondestructive workflow; it does this by providing us with a simple and easily expandable CustomBrush_Landmass Blueprint Brush.

The Blueprint Brush Tool is available next to the other Sculpting Brushes in the Landscape Mode. If you don't see it there, then either the Landmass Plugin is not enabled and or the Enable Edit Layers setting is not activated on your terrain. By clicking the Blueprint Brush Tool icon, we are able to set a couple of properties in the Landscape menu, most importantly, we want to set the Blueprint Brush parameter. There are three options here by default, these are:

- **CustomBrush_Landmass** – This brush is what you will use for creating most landscape shapes.
- **CustomBrush_Landass_River** – This brush we can use for plotting the course of a river although this has been superseded by Epic's water tools which we have explored in Chapter 7.

DOI: 10.1201/9781032663883-8

- **CustomBrush_MaterialOnly** – This brush allows you to use Displacement maps to drive large changes in the Landscape. This is very useful if you are looking to combine other DCC applications with Unreal to produce quick and detailed landmarks.

What isn't obvious with the three default tools is that because these are Blueprints, they can be duplicated and copied between projects. This means it's perfectly possible to create a library of Landscape shapes that you can migrate between projects. This ability alone means it's worth the time to create interesting defaults to help speed up your Landscape creation in all of your projects.

## Creating Your First Landmass Brush

Let's now explore the setup of your first Custom Landmass Brush.

1. Check that your Landscape is close to 0,0,0. Whilst this isn't an ultimate requirement, you may find the placement of brushes easier to control when getting started.
2. Navigate to the **Content Browser**. Open the **Content | Maps** folder and Double Click on the **Landscape_Landmass_Start** level.
3. Enable the **Landscape Mode** and select the **Sculpt** options.
4. Click on the **Blueprint Brush**.
5. Set the **Blueprint Brush** parameter to **CustomBrush_Landmass** and Left Click on your Landscape in the Viewport. You will now see a pyramid shape appear in your world.
6. Note that this can take a few seconds to happen and it's worth zooming out a fair bit initially. An example of shape can be seen in Figure 8.1.
7. If your Brush is too large, try lowering the **Falloff Width** from *8192* to *512* and raising the **Falloff Angle** to *75*. Figure 8.2 shows the Landmass Brush at a more useful size.

Once a Landmass Brush is placed in the viewport we have three types of controls,

- **Brush Placement** – If we select the Brush in the **World Outliner**, we can drag the brush around the entire Landscape using the **Transform** toolset.

**FIGURE 8.1**   Our first landmass brush.

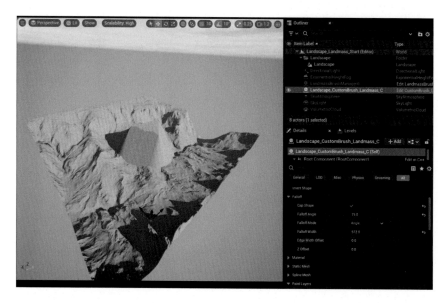

**FIGURE 8.2**  Scaled down brush.

- **Spline Shape Manipulation** – We can manipulate the shape of the Brush by selecting any of the white spline points and moving them individually. We can even add further spline points by selecting spline points at either the start or end of the spline and holding ALT while dragging the Left Mouse button. Each time you select or create a spline point, you also have the option to manipulate the handles of the point to soften the tangent. This can allow you to quickly block out complex shapes.

- **Parameter Setting** – Our last control is via the **Details** panel. There are hundreds of options we can manipulate to adjust the shape, texture and overall appearance of our brush. You will spend most of your time on this menu.

In most situations, you will use all three of the control types listed, initially you will work with brush placement and then manipulate the spline to achieve a suitable shape for the overall Brush before using the parameters to create the unique details and Landscape features. We are now going to review the Details Panel section.

## Exploring the Landmass Brush Details Panel

In this section, we are going to explore some of the options of our Custom Landmass Brush.

One of the most effective and easily accessible options in the Curl Noise. It works exactly like the Water Body Actors in Chapter 7. Two Curl Noises are available to us in the Details panel, we can use one, a combination of both or neither. To use them, we need to put a value greater than 0 into either **Curl 1 Strength** or **Curl 2 Strength**. These strength parameters link to **Curl 1 Tiling** and **Curl 2 Tiling**, we recommend a mixture of larger and smaller tiling amounts to help break up basic shapes. Figure 8.3

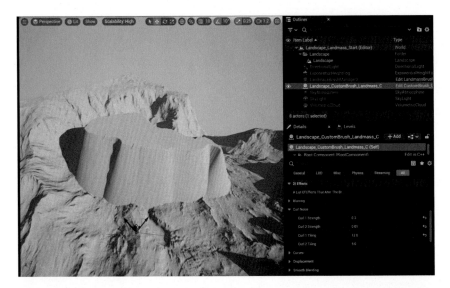

**FIGURE 8.3**   Curl noise.

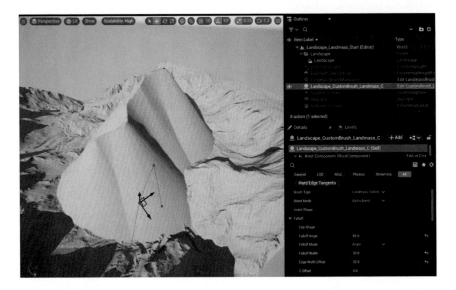

**FIGURE 8.4**   Experimenting with falloff and cap shape.

demonstrates the effect of noise on a Landmass brush with three spline points. Be careful with noise, it can be easily overdone, try to be subtle.

The **Falloff** parameters offer a great deal of flexibility to Landmass Brushes. **Falloff Mode** *Angle* can be useful for quite sharp mountain sides and **Falloff Mode** *Width* for more subtle forms. In addition, we also have float values for **Falloff Width** and **Edge Width Offset**, lower values tend to help reinforce sharper forms and higher values will result in softer features. Figure 8.4 shows how the sides of the mountain have been made sharper by tweaking the falloff parameters.

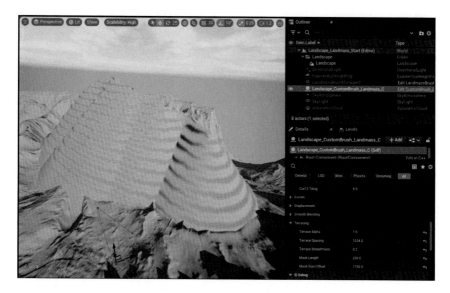

**FIGURE 8.5**   Terracing.

Some landscapes may require visible strata or terracing. We have the ability to also add this into Landscape brushes. By default, the effect is turned off as **Terrace Alpha** is set to 0, dial this up to *1* to allow the **Terracing** parameters take effect.

As with many of the options in this chapter the numbers shown in images are very much trial and error often based on object size. Don't worry too much if the values differ when you try them on your own assets.

Figure 8.5 shows Terracing applied to the Landmass Brush. **Terrace Spacing** controls the gaps between terraces on the Landmass Brush. **Mask Length** at high values will blur the terraces and at low values help reinforce the terraces. We also have to use **Mask Start Offset**, as the Brush isn't based at zero, if this is not set, the mask and terraces are not drawn. Terracing requires a bit of trial and error with these three aforementioned values to get started.

Another great set of options to use is the Displacement Parameters. Here, we can break up the surface of the Brush by repeating a Displacement Texture over it. In Figure 8.6, we've set up the default *TilingNoise5* texture to add some needed variation to the terraces. Many of the Parameters listed here will sound familiar if you've built the Materials earlier on in the Book. The **Displacement Height** value controls the distance that geometry is moved by the texture. The **Tiling Value** is how often the Texture repeats it's details across mesh UVs. Lastly, we can control the **Midpoint** value of the displacement if we wish to ignore a certain range of pixel brightness.

With all of the parameters adjusted, we can now move the Landmass Brush into the background, as shown in Figure 8.7. If we wanted to use this Brush across other areas of the Landscape, we could duplicate the Landmass brush, Move and Rotate the new brush and place it into position.

One of the truly great things about Landmass is that nothing is ever final, we can always adjust parameters, transforms and appearance.

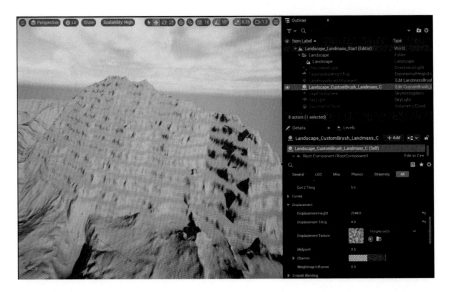

**FIGURE 8.6**   Displacement textures.

**FIGURE 8.7**   Background brush.

## Creating Our Second Landmass Brush

We are now going to showcase another Landscape Brush. This time the result of the Brush is to create a more traditional Mountain Peak that rises from our Landscape base. We will leverage some stronger displacement and less terracing to give the impression of detailed eroded cliff faces. Let's get started!

1. Follow the instructions from earlier in the chapter to create a Brush and place the new Brush on top of the landscape.

2. Select the new Landscape Brush, you can rename them if you wish. Otherwise Unreal will use the convention **Landscape_CustomBrush_Landmass_C**. This can get a little confusing if you have different types of brushes in a large world.

3. First, set **Falloff Angle** to be quite high at *75*. This will create steep slopes.

4. Set the **Falloff Width** and **Edge Width Offset** to *512*, this will add some blending with the base landscape but not too much.

5. Disable **Cap Shape**.

6. Lower the **Z** position of the Brushes **Location** so that it's not too tall. Initially, it may look like a giant wedge of cheese.

7. Next, add some Curl Noise. Set **Curl 1 Strength** to *1* and **Curl 2 Strength** to *0.5*. Then change **Curl 1 Tiling** to *4* and **Curl 2 Tiling** to *8*. This should breakup the perfect shape of the wedge.

8. Lastly, let's add a lot of Displacement. Set the **Displacement Height** to *4096* and the **Displacement Tiling** to *4*. If you can still see Terracing from the previous Brush, set the **Terrace Alpha** to *0*.

9. Review your progress using Figure 8.8, The Mountain brush is a lot taller than the Terrace version. It's also been moved into the backdrop on the opposing side to showcase the difference in structure.

## Creating a Landmass Material Brush

We are now going to try something different. The two previous brushes relied upon manipulating a lot of properties and manipulation of splines to control shape and size.

**FIGURE 8.8** Large displacement values.

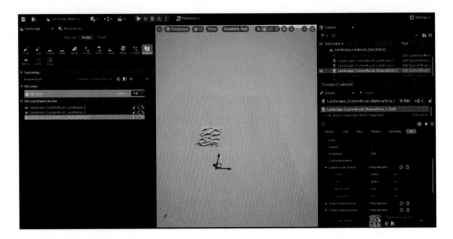

**FIGURE 8.9**   Creating a landmass material brush.

In this next example, we'll rely more on an existing texture. If you have ever painted with stencils you'll find this process somewhat similar. The idea here is that we would create a library of terrain patterns/styles and then paint them onto a Landscape like an artist's canvas. There are many notorious examples of this in the FAB Marketplace, but let's create our own example brush!

1. Enable the **Landscape Mode** and select the **Sculpt** options.
2. Click on the **Blueprint Brush**.
3. Set the **Blueprint Brush** parameter to **CustomBrush_MaterialOnly** and left click on your Landscape in the Viewport.
4. Figure 8.9 shows the result of this Brush application. A flat plane has appeared and the rest of our Landscape appears to have gone aside from a noisy texture in the middle. Do not be alarmed… yet.
5. Scroll down to the **Custom Scalar Params.**
6. Set the **Height** of our Brush to *25000* (this will depend on your own terrains size).
7. Update the **Size** to be *15000*.
8. Raise the **Alpha Falloff** to *0.15*, this will create a greater blend with the landscape. This value can be tweaked quite a lot to create what's needed.
9. Now we need to load in a **Displacement** texture. Locate the parameter **CustomTextureParams**.
10. Replace the **Displacement** parameter with the following texture *Textures | Landscape | Hill.*
11. You should then see a similar result to Figure 8.10.

Figure 8.11 shows the rough overall placement of all three Brushes we've made. You can continue to duplicate these, try different textures and settings to create further unique effects. The great thing with all of these is that the properties and noises can

**FIGURE 8.10** Landmass material brush parameters.

**FIGURE 8.11** Viewing our landmass brushes.

be applied to all of the brushes, even the Material type, to further add detail and interest. The final ultimate victory here is that during a sprint review or art critique when an art director requests you move a mountain or part of a Landscape, you can easily move them, in real time, if you've used these brushes. Try experimenting with the toolset and building a library of different patterns such as rolling hills, sand dunes, canyons and more.

## Conclusion

In this chapter, we've learnt about Parametric creation of Landscape features, using Unreal's powerful Landmass Toolset. We have utilized the Details panel to create complex Landmass Brushes manipulating shape, falloff, noise, displacement and more. This workflow is a great way of kick starting a nondestructive detailed workflow in Unreal; however, we could improve it further with complex erosion and weathering.

At this moment in time, complex erosion and weathering features require other DCCs such as Worldmachine, Houdini and Gaea. For that reason, you may like to try another workflow in addition to what's been demonstrated in this chapter. We recommend you also explore the creation of block outs in Unreal and then further processing happens in a DCC. To do this, you will need to Export your Unreal Landscapes Heightmap using the Landscape Mode's Import/Export features. This process will allow you to bake out your work in Unreal so that additional processing can occur in other packages. Workflows like this allow you to easily progress from block out to a further detailed Landscape. Combining workflows like this is what makes Unreal invaluable as it's able to leverage other software to make its own result even stronger!

The brushes we've created with Landmass worked in two main ways. First, Landmass Material Brushes which have allowed us to place very detailed Textures and second, Landmass Custom Brushes which are great for more simplistic larger forms. You will find several Marketplace tools that further extend the Landmass Material workflow allowing you to paint alpha texture terrains. This feature is fantastic if you can build up a library of Alpha textures. If you are able to combine Landmass Material brushes with a good Landscape Auto Texturing Material you will be able to realize very detailed terrains quickly.

In Chapter 9, we'll continue this nondestructive and procedural approach to art generation as we introduce Unreal's PCG system. We'll use this system to further explore what we can generate and build for our landscapes. These tools should never be seen as the easy route but as a supportive toolset to help you try ideas quickly and iterate.

Before we move on, let's try the chapter quiz!

## Chapter 8 Quiz

Question 1: What is the main advantage of Landmass?

    a. Landmass allows us to build taller mountains which can help us build better alpine levels.

    b. The Landmass Brush system is more efficient than the standard brush tools and runs faster in game.

    c. The Landmass Brush system is non-destructive, we can adjust Blueprint brushes and their properties across a Landscape actor without losing work.

Question 2: What is the benefit of creating our own Landmass Brushes?

    a. It's more efficient.

    b. The default brushes get lost.

    c. We can build up a library of regularly used presets.

Question 3: What setting must be enabled when creating a Landscape to support Landmass Tools?

  a. Enable Edit Landmass.

  b. Enable Edit Layers.

  c. Edit Landmass Enable.

Question 4: Other than creating Landscape Details like Mountains or Valleys what are the other two options Landmass Brushes afford us?

  a. Landmass Brushes can also be used for affecting Landmass Materials and creating Rivers.

  b. Landmass Brushes can be used for streaming levels and buildings.

  c. Landmass Brushes can be used for placing decals and foliage.

## Answers

Question 1: c

Question 2: c

Question 3: b

Question 4: a

# 9

## Introduction to Procedural World Decoration

## Introduction to Procedural World Decoration

In this chapter, we'll explore Unreal's Procedural Content Generation Framework (PCG). The PCG toolset provides additional features to build on Blueprint and other existing engine systems to produce incredibly intuitive tools, buildings, biomes and much more.

If you have experience with other Procedural DCCs such as Houdini, you'll see similarities in Unreal's approach. We'll first look at the fundamentals of enabling Unreal's tools and then move onto some exercises to try. To utilize the tools, you first need to enable the Procedural Content Generation Framework plugin from the Plugins Menu. On most projects, this will require the project to be restarted so make sure you have saved any changes.

The PCG system is driven by Points, these are locations sampled by the PCG system. Points contain lots of attribute information, which we can manipulate in our Graphs. Almost all of the systems, we create will focus on manipulating Points before completing an action such as Spawning a Mesh.

There are two main ways of visualizing our systems Points. One is to use the Debug Mode of a node, this will show any points created at a specific location in a system. The points created are represented with squares in the viewport that showcases their Density (0 is black and 1 is white). The other way of exploring Point information is via Inspecting. When enabling Inspect Mode on a node, we can then review all of the points in a system using the Attributes table.

Let's now look at the main PCG workspace, the Procedural Content Graph.

## Procedural Content Graph

The Procedural Content Graph is where most of our work will take place. Much like other node-based systems, we will work from left to right placing nodes to complete a calculation or series of operations. To view the graph, we first need to make a PCG asset. We can do this in the Content Browser by right clicking and selecting PCG Graph from the PCG Menu. Once an asset has been created, we need to give it a name and press Enter. We suggest that any PCG assets have the prefix PCG_ prior to any name, for example, PCG_RockGenerator.

Double clicking the PCG Asset in the Content Browser will then open the PCG Graph. The Interface can be seen in Figure 9.1, It is split up into six main parts. These are as follow.

DOI: 10.1201/9781032663883-9

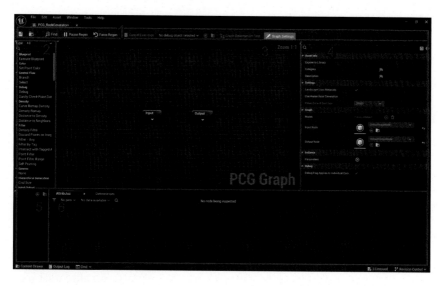

**FIGURE 9.1**  PCG interface.

1. Toolbar
2. Node Palette
3. Viewport/PCG Graph
4. Details Panel
5. Debug Tree
6. Attributes List

The Viewport and Details panel are where most of the work will take place. You can drag and drop nodes into the Viewport/Graph, however, it's often quick to Right Click and search for a node. As you progress and begin to build more complex systems, you'll start to bring the Attributes List and Debug Tree into your workflow.

## PCG Actors

There are two main ways of executing/running a PCG Graph in our worlds, the options are to either use a PCG Volume Actor, placed in the world, or to add a PCG Component to a Blueprint. The PCG Volume Actor can be created via the Place Actors Menu or by simply dragging a PCG Graph Asset into a Level. Drag and Dropping is great as it auto assigns the graph to the actor for you. The PCG Component is a great option when you are building a tool that is more complex, for example, if your PCG system references other Blueprint functions or components, then it's wise to add this in as a component.

When working with PCG Volume Actors specifically, you'll gain access to three new editor functions at the top of the Details panel. These are Generate, Cleanup and Clear PCG Link. Generate will run the PCG Graph and return the results. Cleanup will remove the solution of the PCG Graph from the current level. Clear PCG Link will convert the actor into a PCG Stamp. Depending on what your graph does, this may bake the result down into Hierarchical Static Meshes that will no longer procedurally update and therefore render much faster. The Clear PCG Link is a destructive step in the workflow as there will be no return, but it's often a very helpful one once you are satisfied with your PCG Graphs output.

## Debugging PCG Attributes

PCG Actors and systems have a few new ways of Debugging which are different to other Blueprint and Unreal Tools. The first option is called Debug, to use this option, you first need a level actor using the PCG Graph you wish to debug. You then need to select the node you wish to debug in the PCG Graph and press D on the Keyboard (you can also Right Click on a node and select Debug from the menu). You'll know straight away that an item is set to debug as a blue circle will appear in the upper left corner of the node. Figure 9.2 shows the Surface Sampler node of a Landscape with Debug enabled, this returns all of the points generated by the node with a density filter applied.

Using Debug in this manner is helpful as it can be a nice way to visualize what your Graph is doing. Sometimes the nodes can be a little abstract, and it's not clear what's going on. Matters can be made worse when things are not appearing or rendering, in this case, try debugging each node along the graph until there is a problem. This should at least help you isolate why points are not being created.

Another option to utilize is called Inspect, which operates in a similar way to Debug. The A key enables Inspect on a node, and again, it can also be selected by Right Clicking on a node. However, simply activating Inspect will not return anything, you need to tell the PCG Graph which actor you want to see information about.

**FIGURE 9.2**    Debug example.

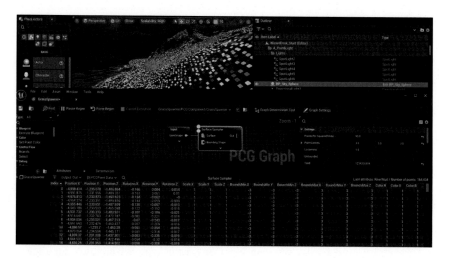

**FIGURE 9.3** Inspect example.

This is easily done by using the drop-down in the center of the PCG Graph UI toolbar and selecting the level actor you want to Inspect.

Figure 9.3 showcases the Attributes inspected from the Landscape Points. The table that's returned is huge and filled with lots of information, this can be a great starting point if you are trying to learn what data is held by a particular actor and what properties you can leverage in your system design. Inspect, for that reason can be leveraged a bit differently to debug, we can use it either to check that our attributes are being applied mid system or we can use it as a research tool to learn about what an actor contains at any time.

## Tree and Rock Spawner

In this exercise, we are going to build our first PCG Graph. It will evaluate our Landscape Actor and create Sampled Points. We will then adjust the Points with a variety of nodes to add things like transformation offsets, noise and pruning before spawning meshes. The overall goal of this first exercise is to understand how Points can be manipulated to our advantage. Let's get started!

1. If you would like to start from an example Open the **Landscape_Procedural_Start** level which can be found in the **Content | Maps** folder. This level has some lighting and very limited foliage.
2. Next, in the **Content Browser** create a folder called **PCG**.
3. Right Click in the **PCG** folder, and from the menu, select **PCG | PCG Graph**.
4. Label the **PCG Graph** asset *PCG_RockSpawner*.
5. Double Click on the **PCG_RockSpawner** asset to open the **PCG Graph Editor**.

6. Next to the **Input** node, Right Click in the PCG Graph, and from the menu, search for the *Surface Sampler* node.

7. Connect the **Input** node's **Landscape** output to the **Surface Input** on the **Surface Sampler**. This will then run some sampling processes on any Landscape our PCG Graph comes into contact with.

8. Next, select the **Surface Sampler** node and navigate to the Details panel. Under **Settings**, adjust the following:
   - Set **Points Per Square Meter** to *1000*.
   - Set **Point Extents** to *25,25,25*.
   - Set **Point Steepness** to *1*.

9. Drag out of the **Surface Sample** node's output, and from the pop-up menu, search for a *Transform Points* node.

10. Select the **Transform Points** node, scroll through the Details panel **Setting** to find the min and max rotational offsets. The values here are arbitrary, and really, you can enter any value you wish. Look for the **Rotation Min** and **Rotation Max** values, ideally, you want to add values that are negative in the Min Parameter and Positive in the Max Parameter. The values here can be thought of as degrees so you could set **Min** to **X**=*-0.5*, **Y**=*-0.5* and **Z**=*-150* and then set **Max** to **X**=*0.5*, **Y**=*0.5* and **Z**=*150*. This will create a large amount of Yaw variation and a small amount of variation on the axes.

11. In addition to Rotation, adding a large amount of **Scale** variation is a good idea to explore. The difference here is that you might want to scale points uniformly rather than adding variation to just one axis. Try setting **Scale Min** to *0.257* on all axes and **Scale Max** to *1* on all axes. By all means return to these values later, if you'd like to try something different.

12. Next, drag out of the **Transform Points** node's output, and from the options menu, search for a *Bounds Modifier* node. Set the **Bounds Max** property to *5* on all axes and set the **Bounds Min** property to *1* on all axes. This makes some points 5 times larger. Inflating points like this is useful for our next operation!

13. Now drag out of the **Bounds Modifier** node's output, and from the options menu, search for a *Self Pruning* node. We can leave the settings as they are, this node will help us remove any points that are too close or similar to each other. This is great for helping us resolve intersections or simply cull the amount of Points where we might have too many.

14. Drag out of the **Self Pruning** node's output and this time search for the *Density Filter* node from the options menu. This node is similar to the pruning node, it allows us to keep Points that have a certain Density value, you can always check this by Debugging a node and checking the Points greyscale value. Try setting the **Lower Bound** to *0.6* and the **Upper Bound** to *0.86*. This will again reduce the amount of points but not based on distance or similarity like pruning.

15. Finally, drag out of the output of the **Density Filter** node, and from the options menu, search for a *Static Mesh Spawner* node.

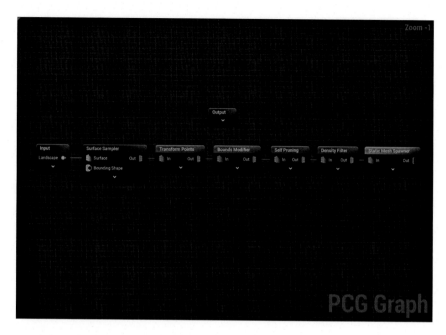

**FIGURE 9.4** Rock spawner PCG graph.

16. Select the **Static Mesh Spawner** node and search for the property **Mesh Entries**. Use the+Button to add an **Array Element** to the **Mesh Entries** Array. Keep expanding the properties until you see the **Descriptor** subsection. In this section, there is a massive amount of properties we can adjust. First, set **Static Mesh** to *Meshes | Pebble_Earth_Mesh* and then disable **Cast Shadow** while we test the system.

17. Review your Graph against Figure 9.4.

18. Save the Graph and Drag a copy of your graph into your open Level. Note that, this Graph will only work on a level with a Landscape as it samples the Landscape to create points. This will create a PCG Volume Actor in the **World Outliner**.

19. Figure 9.5 shows the rocks spawned on the Landscape, however, the PCG actor appears huge, covering a large amount of the Landscape.

20. To control the Rock Spawners exact size, select the PCG Volume Actor, and reset the **Transform Scale** to *1,1,1*. Then scroll down the properties to find **Brush Settings**. Here you can set the X and Y sizes of the PCG Volume to whatever you desire. In Figure 9.6, the settings have been altered to 2000 units. This allows you to create a PCG Volume of an exact size instead of covering most of the level.

With rocks successfully spawning on the Landscape, we'll now look at adding trees into the PCG Graph. While doing this, we want to add some variation of the logic, for example, the trees shouldn't spawn on top of the rocks. More importantly,

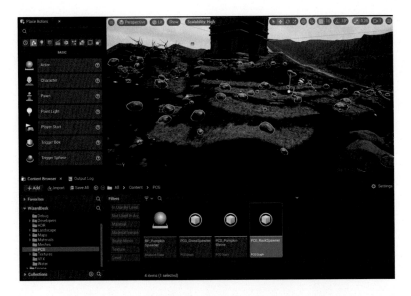

**FIGURE 9.5**   Rock spawner PCG volume in the world.

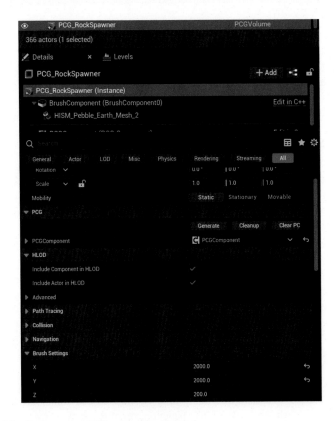

**FIGURE 9.6**   Rock spawner PCG volume details panel.

we also want the trees to grow upward and not simply conform to the Landscape like the rocks. Tree's and certain foliage types can look quite bizarre if their rotation isn't absolute and pointing toward the sun.

Let's get cracking!

1. Just under the existing **Surface Sampler** node, Right Click in the **PCG Graph,** and from the menu, search for the *Surface Sampler* node.

2. Next, select the new **Surface Sampler** node and navigate to the Details panel. Under **Settings** adjust the parameters shown below, this creates larger and fewer points than in the sampler we created for the rocks. Lowering the Steepness values also prevents the trees from spawning on cliffs.
   - Set **Points Per Square Meter** to *25.*
   - Set **Point Extents** to *55,55,55.*
   - **Set Point Steepness** to *0.55.*

3. Drag out of the **Surface Sample** node's output, and from the pop-up menu, search for a *Transform Points* node.

4. Select the **Transform Points** node, scroll through the Details panel **Settings**. Look for the **Rotation Min** and **Rotation Max** values, set **Min** to **X**=*0,* **Y**=*0* and **Z**=*−360* and then set **Max** to **X**=*0,* **Y**=*0* and **Z**=*360.* Also *enable* **Absolute Rotation** to ignore any of the sampled surface rotation, this will ensure the trees face upward with a large amount of Yaw variation.

5. Let's also add a large amount of **Scale** variation. Set **Scale Min** to *0.3* on all axes and **Scale Max** to *1* on all axes. By all means, return to these values later if you'd like to try something different.

6. Next, drag out of the **Transform Points** node's output, and from the options menu, search for a *Bounds Modifier* node. Set the **Bounds Max** property to *2.6, 2.6, 4* and set the **Bounds Min** property to *1* on all axes.

7. Now drag out of the **Bounds Modifier** node's output, and from the options menu, search for a *Self Pruning* node.

8. Drag out of the **Self Pruning** node's output, and this time, search for the *Density Filter* node from the options menu. Set the **Lower Bound** to *0.6* and the **Upper Bound** to *0.86.*

9. Finally, drag out of the output of the **Density Filter** node, and from the options menu, search for a *Difference* node. Ensure the Tree flow of nodes is connected to the **Source Input** of the **Difference** node.

10. Connect the **Rock Density Filter** node's output into the **Differences** input of the **Difference** node. Then Select the **Difference** node and change the **Density Function** to *Binary.* We have now created a Node that will turn off points where the Rocks are spawned.

11. If you debug the **Difference** node, you will see potential Tree placement points such as those shown in Figure 9.7.

12. Finally, drag out of the output of the **Difference** node, and from the options menu, search for a *Static Mesh Spawner* node.

13. Select the **Static Mesh Spawner** node and search for the property **Mesh Entries**. Use the+Button to add an **Array Element** to the **Mesh Entries** Array. Keep expanding the properties until you see the **Descriptor** subsection. Now set **Static Mesh** *Meshes | Tree_Mesh* and then disable **Cast Shadow** whilst we test the system.

14. Save the PCG Graph, you should now see the Trees spawn in the world, as shown in Figure 9.8.

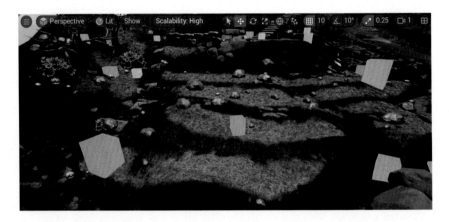

**FIGURE 9.7**    Tree points.

**FIGURE 9.8**    Trees in the level.

We have now completed our first PCG Graph, there's loads we could do to improve it. Some quick ideas you could explore to take this further: First, the tree's roots can sometimes float above the ground, can you find a way to lower the trees into the landscape? Second, the trees and rocks collide with other world geometry. Think about what you could do to ensure there are no random collisions with nonprocedural foliage?

## Grass Spawner

In this example, we are going to create a Graph that will cover an area with lots of grass meshes. It will build on and use many of the nodes from the previous example, however, we have a major design difference; we want our grass to only appear in certain places. Layers like Stone and Mud, for example, should show pebble meshes or other contextual meshes and not grass. To do this, we will explore how we can read attributes into a PCG Graph to tailor mesh spawning.

Let's get started!

1. Continue with the same level or reopen the Landscape_Procedural_Start level if you wish to work from fresh.
2. Next, in the **Content Browser** create a folder called **PCG.**
3. Right click in the **PCG** folder, and from the menu, select **PCG | PCG Graph.**
4. Label the new **PCG Graph** asset *PCG_GrassSpawner.*
5. Double Click on the **PCG_GrassSpawner** asset to open the PCG Graph Editor.
6. Next to the **Input** node, Right Click in the **PCG Graph**, and from the menu, search for the *Surface Sampler* node.
7. Connect the **Input** node's **Landscape** output to the **Surface Sampler** node's **Surface** Input. This will then run some sampling processes on any Landscape our PCG Graph comes into contact with.
8. Next, select the **Surface Sampler** node and hover over to the Details panel. Under **Settings** adjust the following, this will create very small points:
   - Set **Points Per Square Meter** to *90.*
   - Set **Point Extents** to *3,3,3.*
   - Set **Point Steepness** to *1.*
9. Drag out of the **Surface Sample** node's output, and from the pop-up menu, search for a *Point Filter* node. This will now look through the Points to find a specific attribute. In our case, we only want the grass to appear where the **Landscape Grass Layer Blend** has been painted.
10. Set the **Operator** value to ≥, then set the **Target Attribute** to *Grass* (this is the name of the layer in Material), set the **Type** to *Float* and the **Float Value** to *0.3.*
11. Drag out of the **Point Filter** node's **Inside Filter** output, and from the pop-up menu, search for a *Transform Points* node.

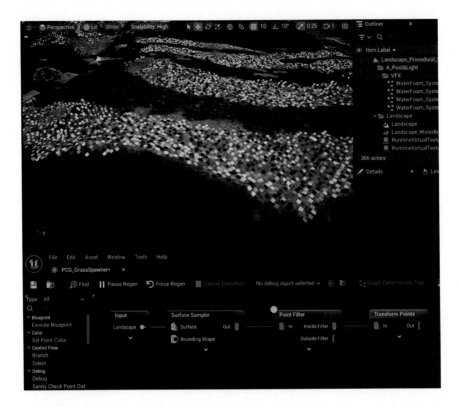

**FIGURE 9.9**  Grass point filter and transformed points.

12. Select the **Transform Points** node, scroll through the Details panel **Settings**. Set **Offset Min** to *0,0,-10* to help place the grass tufts slightly in the level. Look for the **Rotation Min** and **Rotation Max** values, set **Min** to **X**=*−5*, **Y**=*−0.5* and **Z**=*−360* and then set **Max** to **X**=*5*, **Y**=*0.5* and **Z**=*360*.

13. Set **Scale Min** to *0.1* on all axes and **Scale Max** to *0.5* on all axes. It's worth Debugging the Points Filter by selecting the node and pressing D, you can then see check your **Filter** and **Transform** properties are working as shown in Figure 9.9.

14. Next, drag out of the **Transform Points** node's output and from the options menu search for a *Bounds Modifier* node. Set the **Bounds Max** property to *3* on all axes and set the **Bounds Min** property to *1* on all axes.

15. Now drag out of the **Bounds Modifier** node's output, and from the options menu, search for a *Self Pruning* node. Increase the **Radius Similarity Factor** to *0.45*.

16. Drag out of the **Self Pruning** node's output, and this time, search for the *Static Mesh Spawner* node.

17. Select the **Static Mesh Spawner** node and search for the property **Mesh Entries**. Use the+Button to add an **Array Element** to the **Mesh Entries Array**. Keep expanding the properties until you see the **Descriptor** subsection. In this section, there is a massive amount of properties we can adjust.

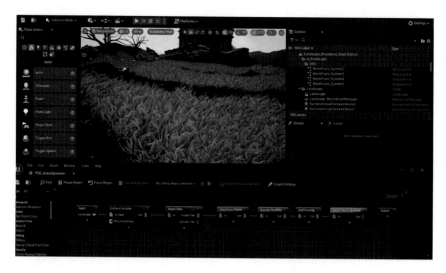

**FIGURE 9.10** Finished grass.

First, set **Static Mesh** to *Meshes | GrassMediumClump1* then disable **Cast Shadow** while we test the system.

18. Save your PCG Graph and compare the results against the finished Graph and example shown in Figure 9.10.

## Pumpkin Spawner

This example will demonstrate how to combine the PCG Graph with Blueprints. This can be very useful as we can leverage components from a Blueprint to alter the results of our PCG Graph. We might want to do this to help control the placement of points and meshes in our world. For example, in a Blueprint, we can add many hundreds of components such as Splines and Collision meshes, which we can then use to communicate with the PCG framework.

The idea behind this next system is that it's drag and drop and requires very little additional tweaking once setup. This creates a prefab like Actor where we create some predefined logic that has some kind of consistency.

The prefab we are aiming to create is a small pumpkin diorama, the Blueprint will create a series of small meshes such as Grass and Rocks and then add in a bigger Pumpkin mesh to finish off. We can leverage the techniques we've already employed in the Rock and Grass Spawners to help build the basis of this Pumpkin Spawner and then add further customization through Blueprint.

Let's get started!

1. Continue with the same level or reopen the Landscape_Procedural_Start level if you wish to work from fresh.
2. Next, in the **Content Browser**, create a folder called **PCG**.

3. Right Click in the **PCG** folder, and from the menu, select **PCG | PCG Graph.**

4. Label the **PCG Graph** asset *PCG_PumpkinSpawner.*

5. Double Click on the **PCG_PumpkinSpawner** asset to open the **PCG Graph Editor**.

6. Next to the **Input** node Right Click in the PCG Graph, and from the menu, search for the *Surface Sampler* node.

7. Connect the **Input** nodes **Landscape** output to the **Surface Sampler** node's **Surface** Input.

8. Next, select the **Surface Sampler** node and hover over to the Details panel. Under **Settings** adjust the following:

   - Set **Points Per Square Meter** to *1000.*
   - Set **Point Extents** to *4,4,4.*
   - Set **Point Steepness** to 0.5.

9. Drag out of the **Surface Sample** node's output, and from the pop-up menu, search for a *Transform Points* node.

10. Select the **Transform Points** node, scroll through the Details panel **Settings**. Set **Offset Min** to *-35,–25,0* and **Offset Max** to *35,25,0.* Look for the **Rotation Min** and **Rotation Max** values, set **Min** to **X**=*5*, **Y**=*–5* and **Z**=*–100* and then set **Max** to **X**=*5*, **Y**=*5* and **Z**=*37.*

11. Set **Scale Min** to *0.08* on all axes and **Scale Max** to *0.5* on all axes.

12. Next, drag out of the **Transform Points** node's output, and from the options menu, search for a *Bounds Modifier* node. Set the **Bounds Max** property to *2* on all axes and set the **Bounds Min** property to *1* on all axes.

13. Now drag out of the **Bounds Modifier** node's output, and from the options menu, search for a *Self Pruning* node. Increase the **Radius Similarity Factor** to **0.25.**

14. Drag out of the **Self Pruning** nodes output, and this time, search for the *Difference* node.

15. Select the **Difference** node and set the **Density Function** Value to *Binary.* We will set the **Difference** node's **Differences Input** later.

16. Drag out of the **Difference** node's output and search for the *Static Mesh Spawner* node.

17. Select the **Static Mesh Spawner** node and search for the property **Mesh Entries**. Use the+Button to add an **Array Element** to the **Mesh Entries** Array. Keep expanding the properties and find the **Descriptor** subsection. Set **Static Mesh** to *Meshes | GrassMediumClump1,* then disable **Cast Shadow**.

18. Underneath the **Surface Sampler** node, Right Click in the **PCG Graph** and from the menu, add another *Surface Sampler* node.

19. Connect the **Input** node's **Landscape** output to the **Surface Sampler** node's **Surface Input**.

20. Next, select the **Surface Sampler** node and navigate to the Details panel. Under **Settings** adjust the following:

- Set **Points Per Square Meter** to *1000*.
- Set **Point Extents** to *10,10,10*.
- Set **Point Steepness** to 0.5.

21. Drag out of the **Surface Sample** node's output and from the pop-up menu search for a *Transform Points* node.

22. Select the **Transform Points** node, scroll through the Details panel **Settings**. Set **Offset Min** to *–35,–25,0* and **Offset Max** to *35,25,0*. Look for the **Rotation Min** and **Rotation Max** values, set **Min** to **X**=*0*, **Y**=*–269* and **Z**=*–100* and then set **Max** to **X**=*0.5*, **Y**=*216* and **Z**=*37*.

23. Set **Scale Min** to *0.08* on all axes and **Scale Max** to *0.5* on all axes.

24. Next, drag out of the **Transform Points** node's output, and from the options menu, search for a *Bounds Modifier* node. Set the **Bounds Max** property to *2* on all axes and set the **Bounds Min** property to *1* on all axes.

25. Now drag out of the **Bounds Modifier** node's output, and from the options menu, search for a *Self Pruning* node. Increase the **Radius Similarity Factor** to *0.25*.

26. Drag out of the **Self Pruning** node's output, and this time, search for the *Difference* node.

27. Select the **Difference** node and set the **Density Function Value** to *Binary*. We will set the **Difference** node's **Differences** Input later.

28. We are now going to drag out of the **Difference** Node's output **two times:**
    1. Drag out and connect to the **Differences Input** of the first **Differences** node.
    2. Drag out and search for the *Static Mesh Spawner* node.

29. Select the **Static Mesh Spawner** node and search for the property **Mesh Entries**. Use the+**Button** to add an **Array Element** to the **Mesh Entries** Array. Keep expanding the properties and find the **Descriptor** subsection. Set **Static Mesh** to *Meshes | Pebble_Earth_Mesh*, then disable **Cast Shadow**.

30. Underneath the second **Surface Sampler** node, Right Click in the PCG Graph and from the Menu search for another *Surface Sampler* node.

31. Connect the **Input** node's **Landscape** output to the **Surface Sampler** node's **Surface** Input.

32. Next, select the **Surface Sampler Node** and navigate to the Details panel. Under **Settings** adjust the following:
    - Set **points Per Square Meter** to *1000*.
    - Set **Point Extents** to *45,45,45*.
    - Set **Point Steepness** to 0.5.

33. Drag out of the **Surface Sample** node's output, and from the pop-up menu, search for a *Transform Points* node.

34. Select the **Transform Points** node, scroll through the Details panel **Settings**. Set **Offset Min** to *–35,–25,0* and **Offset Max** to *35, 25,0*. Look for the **RotationMin** and **RotationMax** values, set **Min** to **X**=*0*, **Y**=*–25* and **Z**=*–300* and then set **Max** to **X**=*25*, **Y**=*216* and **Z**=*360*.

35. Set **Scale Min** to *0.5* on all axes and **Scale Max** to *0.5* on all axes.

36. Next, we are going to create two **Bounds Modifier** nodes. Drag out of the **Transform Points** node's output, and from the options menu, search for a *Bounds Modifier* node. Set the **Bounds Max** property to *1.3* on all axes and set the **Bounds Min** property to *1* on all axes. Then, connect this **Bounds Modifier** to the **Differences** Input on the second **Differences** node we created earlier.

37. Drag out of the **Transform Points** node's output again and search for another *Bounds Modifier* node. Set this node's **Bounds Max** property to *5* and **Bounds Min** property to *1*.

38. Now drag out of the **Bounds Modifier** node's output and search for the *Static Mesh Spawner* node.

39. Select the **Static Mesh Spawner** node and search for the property **Mesh Entries**. Use the +Button to add an **Array Element** to the **Mesh Entries** Array. Keep expanding the properties until you see the **Descriptor** subsection. Set **Static Mesh** to *Meshes | Pumpkin_Mesh.Pumpkin_Mesh* then disable **Cast Shadow**.

40. Save and try the Graph out in the world, your work should look similar to Figure 9.11.

We've now created three chains that end with Static Mesh Spawners. Your Graph should go from Grass, Rocks, and then finally Pumpkins. The problem we have at the moment is the graph takes over the scene very easily and creates too many meshes. We could rescale the PCG Volume which will improve this but we can be smarter!!!

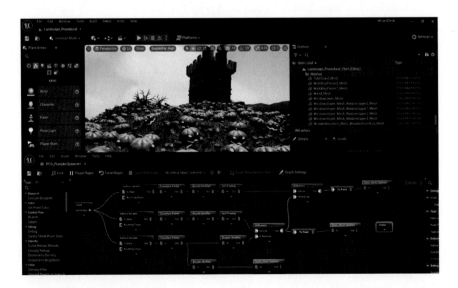

**FIGURE 9.11**   Let there be pumpkins!

We are now going to add a couple of more nodes to the PCG Graph to allow it to read in some Blueprint components and then we shall add the graph to the Blueprint.

1. Delete your **PCG Volume** from the **World Outliner** that has spawned all the Pumpkins.
2. Then move over to the **Input** side of the graph.
3. Right Click in the graph and search for the *Get Primitive Data* node.
4. Drag out of the **Primitive Data** node and search for the *Filter by Tag* node.
5. Select the **Filter by Tag** node, set the **Operation Value** to *Removed Tagged* and set the **Selected Tags** to *Extents*. This will ignore any Primitive component with the tag Extends, this will make sense in a bit!
6. Now drag out from the **Filter by Tag Node** three times and connect it to the **Bound Shape** input on all three **Surface Sampler** Nodes.
7. Now Save your PGC Graph.

Let's now create the Blueprint Actor to control where the Pumpkins Spawn. If you have never used Blueprint before, it is Unreal Engine's visual scripting language. We won't need to do any complex scripting at this point, we'll just create a couple of Components that will be used by the PCG Graph.

1. Right click in the **PCG** folder and from the menu select **Blueprint Class**.
2. From the pop-up menu, click **Actor**, to set the **Parent Class** of the **Blueprint**.
3. Set the name of the **Blueprint** to be *BP_PumpkinSpawner*, then double click the Blueprint Actor to open the **Blueprint Editor**.
4. Using the **Components** list in the top left corner click the **add** button, and from the menu, add a *PCG Component*.
5. With the **PCG Component** select, use the Details Panel far right and set the **Graph value** to be *PCG_PumpkinSpawner*.
6. Now return to the **Components** list and add a *Box Collision* from the menu.
7. Select the **Box** Component and set its **Box Extents** to be *256* in all axes.
8. Press the **Compile** button on the Toolbar and **Save** the Blueprint.
9. Now Drag and Drop the Blueprint from the **Content Browser** into the **Level**. You should see the same results as Figure 9.12.
10. Reopen the **BP_PumpkinSpawner** if you closed it by Double Clicking on the asset in the **Content Browser**.
11. Now, return to the **Components** list and add a **Capsule Collision** from the menu. Set the **Capsule Half Height** and **Radius** to *128* and compile.
12. You should see no visual change, because the **PCG Graph** is pulling shape from the largest primitive extents.
13. Select the **Box Collision Component** in **BP_PumpkinSpawner**. Use the Details panel and search for the property **Component Tag**. Then add an **Array Element** and set the **Component Tag Index [0]** value to be *extents*. The spelling here must match the **Filter by Tag** node spelling in the PCG Graph exactly.

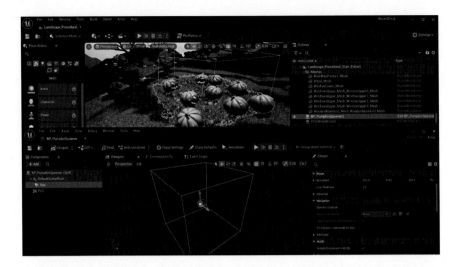

**FIGURE 9.12**    Pumpkin blueprint testing.

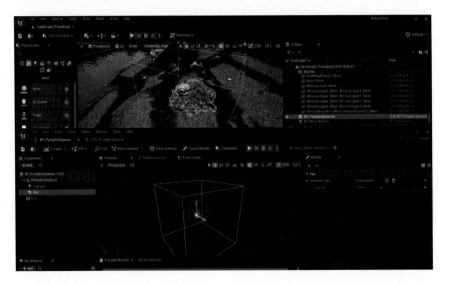

**FIGURE 9.13**    Tagging collision components.

14. Now recompile by pressing the **Compile** button again, you should see that the viewport has been updated to match the shape of the Capsule Collision as shown in Figure 9.13. We now have a simple way of using tags to filter out certain shapes from Blueprints. This is incredibly powerful as we could use some collisions to spawn buildings, for example, or even roads.

15. **Save** and close both the **PCG Graph** and **BP_PumpkinSpawning** Blueprint Editor.

That concludes this exercise, we've been able to spawn many meshes in one Graph and leverage external components to help generate points on a Landscape. One thing to note is that if you have only one Collision Component in Unreal Engine 5.3 you cannot Filter it by Tag in the approach we've used here. The Filter approach works when you are working with multiple Blueprint Components.

## Conclusion

In this chapter, we've worked with Unreal Engine's new PCG toolset, we've learnt how to sample and manipulate points. Starting from Landscape Actors, we've learnt how we can spawn both singular and multiple meshes using different spawn approaches. We've manipulated mesh bounds and utilized pruning to help minimize intersection and generate working Landscape decoration.

To take this teaching further, we recommend looking into Shadow and World Position Offset culling in the Static Mesh spawners to add in some optimization. One of the challenges with these procedural systems is that they can generate massive amounts of meshes and slow down if checks and balances are not implemented. Just because we can does not mean we should.

In addition to foliage, you may wish to look into structures and buildings, all of which can be placed and scattered using the PCG's points system. It's worth trying to plan these systems beforehand, don't be afraid of drawing diagrams of how you think the logic might work before attempting creation in Unreal.

In Chapter 10, we'll carry on with our Material development and explore Automatic Materials for Landscape. Before we move on, let's look at this chapter's quiz!

## Chapter 9 Quiz

Question 1: What does PCG stand for?

    a. Pretty Cool Graph.

    b. Procedural Content Generation.

    c. Position Color Gradient.

    d. Procedural Creation Graph.

Question 2: What is the Attributes List used for in the PCG Graph?

    a. Reviewing what data points from inspected nodes.

    b. Reviewing what Parameters we've created for the PCG Graph.

    c. It lists the PCG Nodes used in our Graph.

Question 3: What does the Clear PCG Link button do in a PCG Volume Actor?

    a. It replaces the PCG Graph in the Actor with a Blank template.

    b. It stops the PCG Volume Actor from updating to any further PCG Graph tweaks and replaces the Actor with a PCG Stamp Actor.

    c. It reverts any recent unsaved changes to the PCG Graph.

Question 4: Which of the following is a common problem when spawning Tree assets via PCG?

   a. Bounds, Careful consideration is needed for the size and shape of a Tree asset to avoid intersection.

   b. Z offset, Tree roots and trunks often need to be sunk into the ground to avoid floating.

   c. Surface normals, if we don't place trees vertically they will grow at odd angles rather than face upward.

   d. All of the above.

## Answers

Question 1: b

Question 2: a

Question 3: b

Question 4: d

# 10

## Auto Landscape Materials

## Auto Landscape Materials

An Auto Landscape Material textures your Landscape automatically without any manual painting. This process runs based on a set of rules that we create in the Material Graph using Math and Logic nodes which automatically blend Landscape Textures. We feed the result into our existing Landscape Material as a single Landscape Blend Layer. The main idea behind this approach is to generate a good working base to begin detailed, manual painting.

The workflow for creating Auto Landscape Materials is to first create a workable painting Landscape Material similar to what we have done in earlier chapters, this gives us the knowledge to control things like RVT, Landscape Tiling, Material Functions and a whole host of parameters. We can then add additional features to create our Automatic Material.

So how do we decide what to add? Automatic Materials usually combine two factors: slope and height. If we consider three simple Landscape Materials: Grass, Rock and Snow, we can very crudely determine where they will be on our Landscape by using the slope and height parameters for example,

- Grass, often found on flat areas and low angle slopes at lower altitudes.
- Rock, often found on angular slopes at medium altitudes.
- Snow, often found on flat slopes at higher altitudes.

The above is a very simple take, we could also factor things like Sun Rise and Fall patterns to increase snow melt, import texture maps from Houdini or Gaea to show complex erosion and add complex water body blends to showcase rivers and lakes, etc. These additional features can add further variation to your world and help improve its realism, however, with each extra step of processing, some game performance will naturally be lost. There is always some balancing to be considered.

We will begin by exploring some nodes that we can manipulate to control Height and also the Slope of the Landscape Actor. You can work within the already developed M_Landscape Master Material or a Landscape Material of your own choosing, the main requirement will be the use of the Landscape Layer Blend node.

Let's get started!

DOI: 10.1201/9781032663883-10

## Masking Height

Our first experiment will be to help figure out how we can obtain the height of our Landscape. We need a way to generate a Black and White Mask based on the position of the vertices of our Landscape. So how can we do this?

1. Open up our **M_Landscape** Material from **Content | Materials | Master** folder. If you have not yet completed this Material, please revisit Chapters 4 and 5 before attempting this.

2. Temporarily break the connections that go from the **Runtime Virtual Texture Sample** node into the **Make Material Attributes** node (this will be quite close to the **Material Results**).

3. Underneath these nodes, Right Click in the **Material Graph** and search for *World Position*.

4. Drag out from the **Absolute World Position** node's **XYZ** pin and search for *Divide* from the pop-up menu.

5. Next, Right Click on the **B** pin on the **Divide** node and select **Promote to Parameter** to create a Scalar Parameter, which is automatically labeled as **B**.

6. Label the new Scalar Parameter *MudHeight*. If you clicked off the node already, you can rename it by selecting it and using the **Details** Panel. Set the **Default Value** to *15000* for now. This represents roughly the height units we want to see.

7. Next, drag out from the **Divide** node and add a *BreakOutFloatComponents 3Node* from the pop-up menu.

8. Then drag out from the **Break Out Float Component** node's **Z** output pin and add a *One Minus* node from the pop-up menu. This will produce only inverted Z values.

9. Lastly, to view the output of this series of nodes connect the **One Minus** into the **BaseColor** and **Emissive** inputs of the **Make Material Attributes** node.

10. Finally, save the material.

You can compare your changes to the material against the example in Figure 10.1, Figure 10.2 shows the effect of the Mask when the **MudHeight** is about 500.

The Height Mask is a really useful way of limiting where a texture appears on a Landscape. You can optimize it further by dragging out of the Absolute World Position Z Output to avoid having to Break the Float apart later on. In addition, you can also soften the falloff between the Black and White values by manipulating the One Minus result with a Power node. There's lots of opportunities here to make the result interesting. One of the most commonly used approaches, however, is to combine the result with a Slope Mask which we'll do next.

## Masking Slopes

In our next experiment, we are looking at the Slope of the Landscape faces. The idea here is that Landscape Layers like Grass may not be present at particular angles. There are a couple of ways of achieving this, we'll focus on the Slope Mask node in a

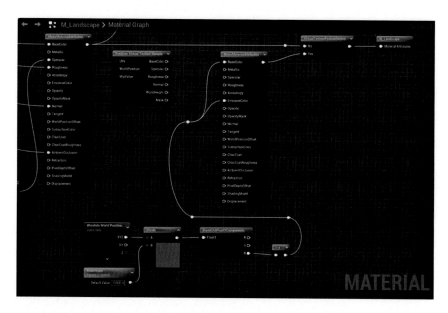

**FIGURE 10.1** Material preview of our mud height mask.

**FIGURE 10.2** Level preview of our mud height mask.

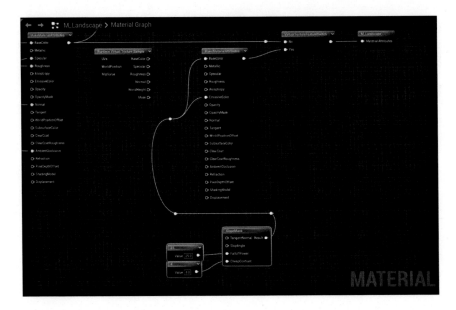

**FIGURE 10.3**    Material preview of our slope mask.

moment but you might also want to try the World Aligned Texture node as a comparison. Let's get building!

1. Cut and paste the nodes we used for the Height Mask shown in Figure 10.1 to the top left of our Material Graph. We will save these for later.
2. Go back to the **Make Material Attributes** node. Right click in the Graph and add a *Slope Mask* node from the pop-up menu.
3. Create two Constants by holding 1 on the keyboard and Left Clicking in the **Material Graph**. Set one of the Constants to a **Value** of *25* and connect this to the **Falloff Power** input pin of the **Slope Mask**. Select the other Constant and set its **Value** to be *4* and then connect this to the **Cheap Contrast** input of the **Slope Mask**.
4. Next, connect the **Result** output of the **Slope Mask** to the **BaseColor** and **Emissive** input pins of the **Make Material Attributes** node.
5. Hit **Save** and compare your progress against the nodes shown in Figure 10.3.

When compared with Figure 10.4, we can see that the nodes produce a Mask that grabs polygon faces that are quite flat, this is great for surfaces like Grass, Snow, and even Sand. But what about polygons that face to the side rather than upwards? We can make two simple changes, try the following:

1. Set the value of the Constant (**25**) that connects to **FallOffPower** to *2*.
2. Set the value of the Constant (**4**) that connects to **CheapContrast** to *5*.
3. Check your settings against Figure 10.5.

**FIGURE 10.4** Level preview of our slope mask.

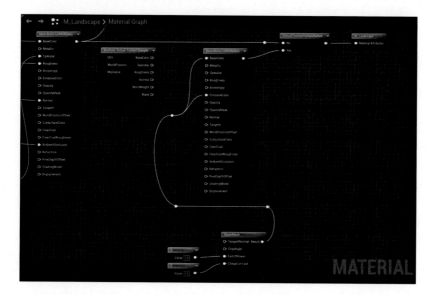

**FIGURE 10.5** Material preview of our slope mask for rocks.

**FIGURE 10.6**   Level preview of our slope mask for rocks.

In Figure 10.6, we can see that all the Stone polygons are painted black. We can now utilize this mask to blend between Rock and Stone.

Before we move on, we need to put a few things back in place from before these experiments:

1. Cut and paste the **Slope Mask** nodes next to the **Height Mask** nodes we made earlier. Again, we will keep these to use later.
2. Reconnect the **RunTime Virtual Texture Sample Outputs** to the **Make Material Attributes Inputs**, this includes BaseColor, Specular, Roughness and Normal.

---

## Blending Setup for Rock and Stone

Our first step is to create a Blend between the MudHeight and Stone SlopMask nodes.

1. Using the nodes we created before, recreate the node structure shown in Figure 10.7. Be mindful to copy the values of the **Constant** and **Scalar Parameters** exactly.
2. Multiply the **Height Mask** and **Slope Masks** nodes together.

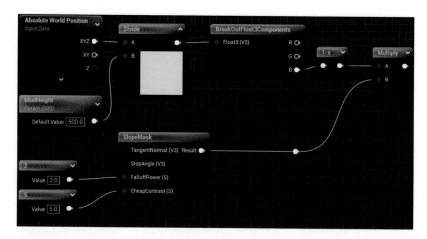

**FIGURE 10.7**   Blending between rock and stone.

**FIGURE 10.8**   Level preview blending between rock and stone.

You don't need to preview the result of this yourself but if you'd like to see what this does to the Landscape please review Figure 10.8. Here, you can see white where our mud texture should be placed and black where the stone texture should be placed. Tweaking The MudHeight or either of the two Constant nodes connected to the Slope Mask will allow you to further tweak the result.

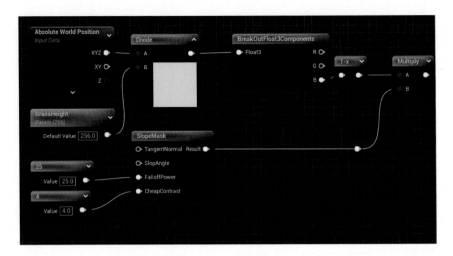

**FIGURE 10.9**   Blending grass and the others.

## Blending Setup for Grass

Now we need to create the Grass result, which is pretty much identical, let's get started.

1. Select the node chains created for the Mud and Stone, Copy and Paste the nodes underneath.
2. Relabel the **MudHeight** Scalar Parameter to *Grass Height* and set its value to *256*.
3. Set the **FalloffPower** constant to *25*.
4. Set the **CheapContrast** constant to *4*.

You can compare your changes to the example in Figure 10.9, which shows the resulting node structure. Figure 10.10 shows the final result of white polygons, which is where our Grass will be applied.

## Connecting It to Our Existing Landscape Material

To connect these masks to our Material and blending nodes, we need to go through and add a few named reroute nodes.

1. Pan to the Mud **MF_LandscapeLayer** Function, drag out of the **Result** pin and add a *Named Reroute* node. Call this *MudLayer*.
2. Now visit the **MF_LandscapeLayerFunction** for **Grass** and **Stone**. Create a *Named Reroute Node* for each material, call them *GrassLayer* and *StoneLayer*.
3. Compare your result against Figure 10.11, which shows the *MudLayer* adjustment.

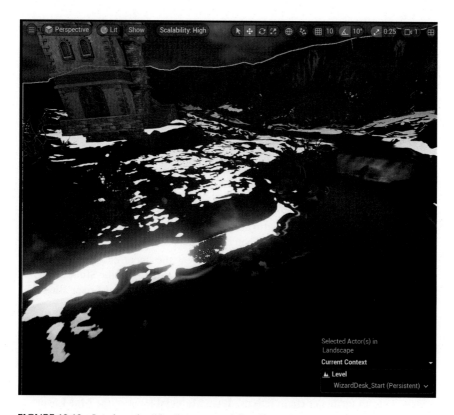

**FIGURE 10.10**   Level preview blending grass and the others.

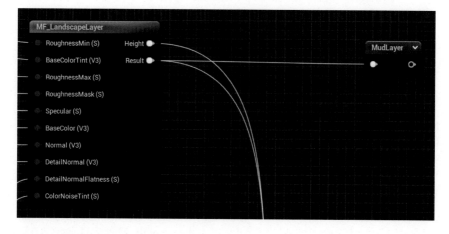

**FIGURE 10.11**   Named routes from our material functions.

This process allows us to copy the result of our Material Functions very quickly to different parts of the graph. We now need to create the rest of the Slope and Height Mask logic now we can access our Material Function outputs easily.

Next, we need to connect the two blend systems together. Be sure to place the MudHeight-driven blend on top and the grass one at the bottom. The nodes can be anywhere in the graph. We suggest top/middle left just to keep things tidy. We are now going to add a few additional nodes to merge the two chains.

1. On both chains, add a **Saturate** node after the **Multiply**. This will limit the values between 0 and 1 which stops any colors which cause strange material blending later on.
2. Next Right Click in the Material Graph and search for the node *MatLayerBlend_Standard*. Copy and paste this node to make a duplicate.
3. Connect the upper chains **Saturate** node output into the **Alpha** of the **Mat Layer Blend Standard** node. Then repeat this process for the lower chain.
4. Next, Right Click in the Material Graph near the upper chain and select *StoneLayer* from the **Named Reroutes** list and then connect the **StoneLayer** output into the **Base Material** input of the upper chains **Mat Layer Blend Standard** node.
5. Now Right Click in the Material Graph near the upper chain and select **MudLayer** from the **Named Reroutes** list and then connect the **MudLayer** output into the **Top Material** input of the upper chains **Mat Layer Blend Standard** node.
6. Connect the **Blend Material** output of the **Mat Layer Blend Standard** node from the upper chain into the **Base Material** input of the **Mat Layer Blend Standard** node from the lower chain.
7. Now Right Click in the Material Graph near the lower chain and select **GrassLayer** from the **Named Reroutes** list and then connect the **GrassLayer** output into the **Top Material** input of the lower chains **Mat Layer Blend Standard** node.
8. Drag out of the lower chains **Blend Material** output from the **Mat Layer Blend Standard** node and add a *Named Reroute* node.
9. Select the **Named Reroute** node and call it *AutoLayer*.

This series of nodes now combines both masking systems with the material functions and provides us with an output called AutoLayer, which we can reuse elsewhere in the Material. It's worth saving the material at this point and comparing your work with Figure 10.12. The color of your Reroute nodes may be different from the example, don't worry if they are. Named Reroute nodes are connected by name, the color is a visual indicator to help us organize our graphs. We now need to connect this work into our existing Landscape Layer Blend system, fortunately, we can expand on what we did in earlier chapters pretty quickly.

To connect our AutoLayer into our Material, we need to create a new input in the Landscape Layer Blend system. I like to do this at the top of the Material Layers Array so all other layers come after this, to do this:

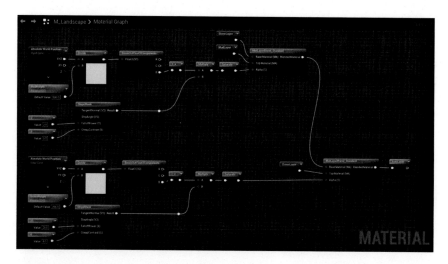

**FIGURE 10.12**   Final height and slope mask blend.

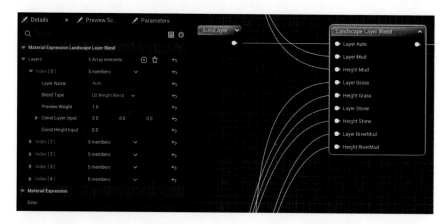

**FIGURE 10.13**   Landscape layer blend.

1. Use the+button next to the **Layers** array in the Details panel and adjust the layers as necessary. An example can be seen in Figure 10.13, the existing connections from our Material Functions still need to be connected.

2. All we need to do is set the **Blend Type** to *LB Weight Blend* for the Auto Layer.

3. Next, Right Click in the Graph and search for the *Auto Layer* named reroute and connect it to your **Landscape Layer Blend** node.

After connecting the Auto Layer to our Landscape Layer Blend node, we can save the Material and jump to the Landscape Mode View. You will need to create a Landscape Layer Info for the new layer like we did in Chapters 4 and 5. Check all the Layers in the Paint options have a layer info assigned and if not create one using the plus button. Figure 10.14 shows what the completed setup looks like.

Your Landscape should now look something like Figure 10.15 which shows the AutoLayers attempt at layering in the three main Landscape Layers. Your result may differ particularly if you've painted a lot on the other terrain layers. You can easily reset them by right clicking on the Layers in the Landscape Mode Paint view and selecting **Clear**.

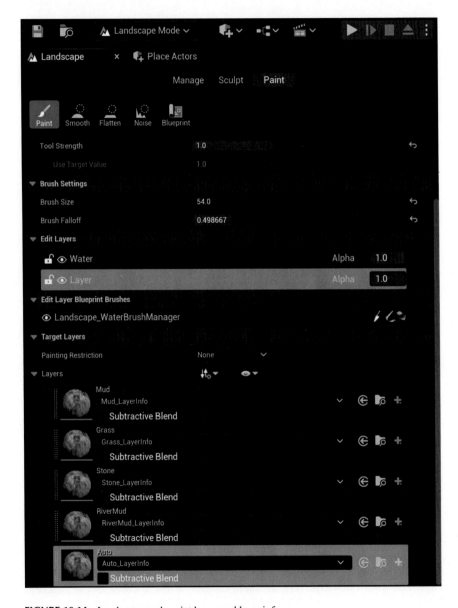

**FIGURE 10.14**   Landscape mode paint layers and layer info.

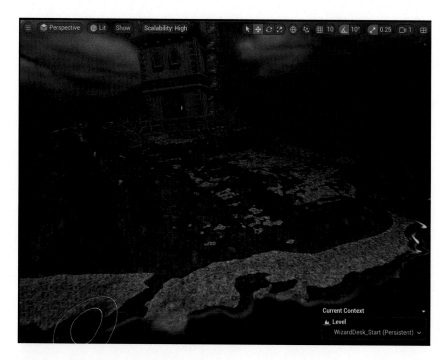

**FIGURE 10.15** Auto landscape result.

One of the issues that comes from the auto texturing is that the effect is quite splotchy in places and often disjointed. You can improve this in a couple of ways such as experimenting with the Slope Mask constants, adding more noise to the texture blends and also painting on top of the Auto Layer using the Paint Tools in the Landscape Mode (my preferred option).

## Corrective Painting

Figure 10.16 shows the start of some corrections. The Landscape Modes paint tools have been used to bridge appropriate areas and blend pockets of grass that make sense. This painting process can take some time, you can speed the process up if you have a nice library of terrain noises and textures to help the painting process. Try to experiment with the falloff and brush alphas if you find the corrective painting is a bit too soft.

Is there anything else we can do? Yes, if you have water bodies/actors in the levels, we can use their toolset to feed into the Material Automatically. You might have noticed that we haven't used the River Mud layer yet. Using Unreal's water tools, we are able to paint a mask where the water actor touches the Landscape creating a river bank effect automatically. How can we try this?

1. Search for the **Layer Weightmap Settings** in any Water actor such as **WaterBodyRiver**.

2. Expand the Map elements using the + button.

3. Add the name *RiverMud*/any LandscapeLayerBlend you wish to paint with.

4. Experiment with the **Falloff** and **Edge Offset** values to create a bank.

5. Load in any **Modulation Texture** as desired.

You may find this takes a bit of time to update in the scene. Reviewing Figure 10.17 you can now see the settings applied, and the riverbank is now shinier/wetter than the surroundings.

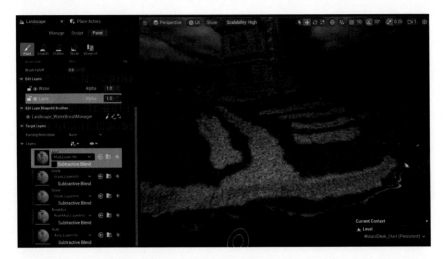

**FIGURE 10.16**   Auto landscape and corrective painting.

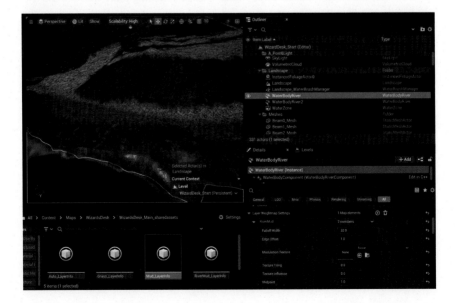

**FIGURE 10.17**   Auto landscape and auto water edge.

It's worth noting that the Water Edge effect can be buggy if your terrain is rotated. If you experience problems you can always resort to manually painting some of the river bed using the RiverMud Paint Layer in Landscape Mode.

## Conclusion

We have now come to the close of our Landscape Material exploits. We've added some final logic to set up auto texturing and also water edge detection. These additional features, while slight, all go hand-in-hand to creating quick Landscape and Lookdev materials.

To push this further, you could resort to using more Material Functions for different terrain layers and look into more complex texture repetition solutions. The basis of the Landscape Material however is highly customizable and provides a good base for you to experiment with.

From here, you should also ensure you connect the Landscape with PCG, Procedural Foliage and or Unreal's Grass system to help auto cover some of the areas of your world. Try to always link what you are doing with other relevant systems to help accrue performance and development gains. In Chapter 11, we'll begin to look at bigger worlds using World Partitions. Before we move on, let's tackle this chapter's quiz.

## Chapter 10 Quiz

Question 1: Why do we use Auto Landscape Materials?

    a. We use Auto Landscape Materials to get a good starting base for Lookdev and Landscape Texturing.

    b. We use Auto Landscape Materials so that cars can drive on the Landscape.

    c. We need to Auto Landscape Materials so that our Landscape Material is rendered Automatically.

Question 2: What are two common factors that go into an Auto Landscape Material?

    a. Slope Mask.

    b. Height Mask.

    c. Salty Mask.

    d. Snow Mask.

Question 3: Why should we consider correcting Auto Landscape Materials?

    a. Auto Landscape Materials need to be saved in a very precise format.

    b. We might need to improve the efficiency of our Landscape.

    c. Blends and Texturing can look quite artificial in places so it's important to add finesse.

Question 4: When applying our Auto Landscape Material to our Landscape Actor what do we need to check?

    a. We need to check that the Landscape has a grass layer.

  b. When our Auto Landscape Material is applied to the Landscape Actor, we must ensure that a LayerInfo has been set up in the Landscape Paint Mode. Otherwise the layer will not appear properly.

  c. We should ensure our level is Rebuilt.

## Answers

Question 1: a
Question 2: a & b
Question 3: c
Question 4: b

# 11

## World Partition

## What Is World Partition?

In this chapter, we are going to explore Unreal Engine's World Partition System. The World Partition System allows us to build large, expansive worlds in a single persistent level, unlike the level streaming approach, we've explored previously which uses multiple levels. World Partition facilitates the creation and exploration of large worlds by dividing the world into a grid, loading each section of the grid (known as cells) based on the distance it is from a streaming source (typically the player).

World Partition isn't something you would typically use if you were working on a project which is focused primarily on visuals. If the aim of your project is to output a series of high-quality renders or screenshots, or perhaps a flythrough video render for a showreel, it's unlikely that you are going to need to have your world dynamically load based on the position of your camera. If you are working on a project which will feature gameplay however, you may find World Partition is very useful for achieving great performance while maintaining control over specific aspects to ensure the player never sees the system working.

## Exploring World Partition

We're going to look at applying World Partition to the example levels, we've provided a little later in the chapter. Before we dive into such a complex world, we can explore the World Partition system using one of the template maps, allowing us to discover firsthand how things work and what options we have as environment artists to control the system.

1. First, we need to create a new level which already has World Partition enabled, to do this navigate to **File | New Level** and select **Open World** from the pop-up and click **Create**.
2. This should open a new level which for now will be labeled as **Untitled**. Save the level with **File | Save Current Level** or CTRL + S. Call the level *World Partition Test* and save it in the **Content | Maps** directory.
3. When you created the level, Unreal may have opened the **World Partition** panel automatically (as shown on the right side of the user interface of Figure 11.1). If not, navigate to **Window | World Partition | World Partition Editor**, this should open the **World Partition** panel in the same UI slow as the **Details** panel.

DOI: 10.1201/9781032663883-11

*165*

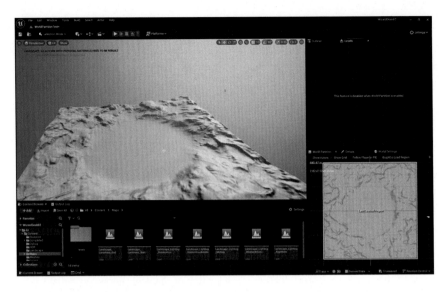

**FIGURE 11.1**    A new open world level with the world partition panel visible.

## The World Partition Editor

The World Partition Editor (which is shown in the World Partition panel) shows you a visual representation of the level in a minimap format (something gamers are more than familiar with) split up into a grid format. The grid itself, however, can be a little misleading. The grid squares that you see in the minimap aren't necessarily how the grid is split up in the world. To get a better understanding, we need to take a closer look at the grid in the minimap first by turning on the Cell Coordinates.

1. In the **World Partition** panel, click the >> icon in the top right corner of the minimap.
2. From the pop-up, enable **Show Cell Coords**.
3. You will notice that nothing about the minimap has changed, and that's because the coordinates aren't visible until you zoom in. Using the Scroll Wheel on your mouse, zoom in until you see the Cell Coordinates appear, as shown in Figure 11.2.
4. Zoom back out for a moment in the minimap and then Left Click in the viewport, this will select one of the **Landscape Streaming Proxy** actors that make up the Open World starter map. Note that when you look at the minimap, you should be able to see a darker outline around the selected actor.

Figure 11.2 also shows a white cursor-like arrow on the zoomed-out version. This denotes the position of the editor viewport camera in the world. When you press the Play button to Play in Editor, the arrow turns orange. This shows the position of the player/viewport in the world, the orange color is a visual indicator to show that we are in Play in Editor mode.

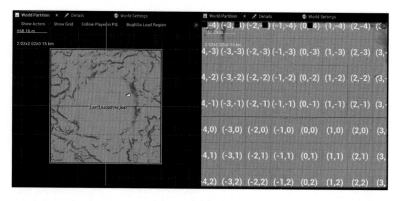

**FIGURE 11.2** The world partition minimap zoomed out and in with cell coordinates enabled.

As default, the grid size shown on the minimap doesn't match the grid size in the world, to see this for yourself, we can do a little experiment:

1. Navigate to the **World Settings** panel, if this isn't visible, you can turn it on by navigating to **Window | World Settings**.
2. Find the **World Partition Setup** section and expand **Runtime Settings**.
3. Enable **Preview Grids**. You should see a grid overlay appear in the viewport, over the top of the landscape. You will also see a circular shape drawn on the landscape, this is a visual representation of the loading distance. Based on the current settings, the light-colored cells of the grid would be loaded, whereas the unshaded ones would not. An example of this can be seen in Figure 11.3, we've exaggerated the circle to make it clearer here, it's only one pixel wide in the viewport which you should be able to see on your screen.
4. Select one of the **Landscape Streaming Proxy** actors again by clicking one in the viewport.
5. Navigate to the **World Partition** panel and locate the selected actor (denoted by a dark gray outline). You will notice that there is an inconsistency between what the minimap is suggesting compared to the overlay.
6. If you zoom in on the minimap you will see the cell coordinates also don't match the grid squares on the Preview Grid.

So why is that? Well, the answer is because the minimap grid and the world grid are set up differently as they support two different uses, an editor workflow and in-game behavior but this can get a little confusing. The editor cell size by default, is set to 12,800 (128 m²), this is half the size of the default World Partition cell, which by default is 25,600 (256 m²). To make things a little easier, we can modify the settings to make the grids match, let's look at how we do that:

1. First, you'll notice that the two grids aren't aligned with their origins. We can change this by setting the **Use Aligned Grid Levels** to *Enabled*. You should see the grid change in the world, it should now appear to match the position of four cells on the minimap.

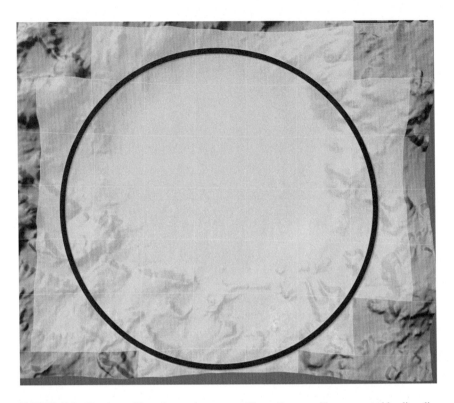

**FIGURE 11.3**   Preview grid overlay on the open world sample map with exaggerated loading distance circle.

2.  To have the grid match the minimap, set the **Cell Size** to half of the default, so *12800*. You can either type in *12800* or you can add */2* to the value, Unreal will do the math for you and update the value. If you now compare the grid squares, you can see in the viewport to the grid squares in the minimap, they should now make a lot more sense.

It's worth noting at this point what we have just done. We have increased the number of subdivisions that World Partition is managing, doubling the previous amount. Selecting the correct values for your world will depend on multiple factors, including the target platform and what type of environment you are working with. If the environment is quite sparse, such as a desert, having small cells won't be beneficial as there may not be many objects in a single cell. If you are working in a built-up suburban environment with lots of houses, cars, fences, lamp posts, etc. you may benefit from having World Partition control those in physically smaller groups.

## World Partition in Action

To get a better sense of what World Partition does, we are going to test it out within the level, add in some static meshes and change some variables to emphasize the effect. Before we do any of that though, we should experience the default behavior.

**NOTE**

The World Partition system is ever evolving so may change significantly between versions of Unreal, as long as you familiarize yourself with how the grid works, it aligning with the minimap is less of a concern, it's functionality and ability to help optimize your levels is the key consideration.

1. In the viewport, Right Click on one corner of the open-world landscape and select **Play From Here** from the pop-up menu.
2. Hold down Right Click and move your mouse to direct the camera and then use W on the keyboard to fly across the map (the default speed is quite slow, sorry). Note how, as you move around, you can see the world popping into existence, this is happening because you, the player/camera, is within the default 76,800 m of the cells you are watching appear and World Partition is loading them and making them visible.
3. To make the effect more obvious, stop the Play in Editor mode by pressing Esc on the keyboard and change the **Loading Range** in the **World Settings** panel to *12800* and repeat the test. You should now see a lot less of the world and the popping in will occur much closer to the camera.
4. Press Esc once more and change the **Cell Size** to *1600* (this is the smallest it will go). This is very small but what you should observe is very little change in the behavior of the landscape loading in. This is because the landscape pieces are all around 25,600 m$^2$ and will load in as soon as a cell which it is within is loaded, so they will behave in the same way as they did before.
5. To prepare for the next experiment, reset the values to their default. which can't be achieved using the reset arrow like most other properties in Unreal, instead you will need to do it manually the **Cell Size** should be *25600*, and the Loading Range should be 76,800.

Now that we've seen the landscape pieces load in as we move around the space (and out again if you moved backward), we should also explore what happens with static meshes as they are physically much smaller in the world compared with the landscape pieces. To do this, we are going to need to add some objects to the level, we're going to use a feature of the Content Browser called Collections, a useful tool for building categories of assets that is useful for things like maintain thematic placement of objects in environments or grouping gameplay features into one place where otherwise they might be scattered around the folder structure. We're going to use a collection to create a collection of meshes we can place which will be suitable for this experiment. The main reason for isolating these meshes is because many of the meshes we've included in the project are physically quite small and will be difficult to see appearing, so we're going to make grabbing the larger ones a bit easier.

1. In the **Content Browser**, navigate to **Content | Meshes**, this is where all of the meshes used to build the example environment are stored.
2. In the bottom left of the **Content Browser**, click the + button next to **Collections** and select **Local Collection**, label the new collection *Placeable*.

3. To add meshes to the collection, we simply locate the mesh in the **Content Browser** and drag and drop it onto the **Placeable** collection name. Do this with the following static mesh assets:

- **StoneFloor_Mesh**
- **ExteriorArchyway0_Mesh**
- **FirePlaceStone_Mesh**
- **StonePillar_Mesh**
- **Tree_Mesh**

4. When you've dragged them all into the **Placeable** collection, click the **Placeable** title, the **Content Browser** window should now swap over to just showing the meshes you dragged in.

5. Now you have them easily selectable, place a random selection of things at one end of the flat plateau in the world.

6. Right Click next to the placed meshes and select **Play From Here**. This time, continue to look at the objects and use S to travel backward away from them. The default behavior should result in the objects disappearing and being unloaded when they are very small on the screen, it's still noticeable because there is no fog or other disguising techniques, but at this distance, the change in visual is quite minimal.

7. The purpose of this section however is to see how they behave differently with smaller Loading Ranges. In the **World Settings** panel, change the **Cell Size** variable back to *1600*, and the **Loading Range** to *12800*. Complete the test from Step 6 again. You should see the meshes disappear long before the landscape tile beneath it, this is due to the size of the object and the fact that the small cell they are in is no longer inside the Loading Range but, because the landscape tile is part of multiple cells, one of those cells is still inside the loading range and keeping the landscape tile visible.

8. Let's put the values back to something sensible, but not their defaults. Set the **Cell Size** to *12800*, this will now match the grid visible in the minimap. Set the **Loading Range** to *38400* which is around half of the usual value. If you test it here, you will still get a similar result due to the landscape tiles sitting in four cells compared to the meshes, which will likely only be inside one or two.

We're going to keep these settings to explore how we can control the visibility of meshes and override World Partition's default behavior. There may be instances where games designers may want to keep certain landmark objects visible at all times, think about how Disney has a castle at the center of each of their amusement parks, these castles are visible from most places in the park and make it easier to work out where you are in relation to the center of the park and help you to keep your bearings in a potentially overwhelming environment. So let's explore how we can do the same with our castle block out from Chapter 2. If you haven't made the castle block out, we have included a BOCastle_Mesh you can use for this exercise.

1. In the **Content Browser**, navigate to **Content | Meshes** and find the **CastleBlockOut_Mesh** asset (or **BOCastle_Mesh**) and drag it onto the map, near one of the corners of the flat plateau.
   - If you want to navigate to a part of the map quickly, you can double click on the minimap.
2. Check that the mesh behaves as you'd expect and disappears as you move away from it. You will need to be near the middle of the map with the current settings.
3. Select the Castle Mesh and in the **Details** panel, search for *World Partition* to show only the World Partition settings for the actor.
4. Uncheck **Is Spatially Loaded**. This will stop World Partition from controlling when the mesh is shown.
5. Test this out again. Now, when you move away, the Castle should remain, no matter how far away you get.

## Working with Multiple Grids

It is possible in World Partition to use multiple grids of different sizes, setting different objects to use different layers and different loading ranges. The benefit of this is that you can set priorities for objects to be loaded, allowing you to set less important objects to load in at closer distances compared with more important elements of the scene. This could be used, for example, to have smaller decorations like litter in a street, load in when you are within a hundred meters of them while keeping things like lamp posts, kerbs, buildings and other more important features of the street loading in when you are much further away.

To set these up you need to do two things, firstly create an additional grid, secondly, assign the objects to the grid.

1. In the **World Settings** panel, locate the **Grids** rollout in **World Partition Setup | Runtime Settings** and click the + icon next to **1 array element**. This will create a second grid.
2. Set the **Grid Name** to *Meshes*, the **Cell Size** to *1600*, and the **Loading Range** to *1600*. These are fairly extreme values but they are here to show the effect, not be overly practical.
3. From the **Placeable** collection, place two **Tree_Mesh** assets into the level.
4. Select just one of the newly placed tree meshes. In the **Details** panel, search for *World Partition* and set **Runtime Grid** to say *Meshes*.
5. Right click in the viewport near the trees and select **Play From Here**.
6. Repeat the usual test, moving away from the trees whilst looking at them, note how one tree (the one you selected in step 4) disappears almost immediately, whereas the other tree takes much longer. This is the effect of using multiple grids in World Partition.

Now that we've explored how World Partition works and what the various parameters control, we are going to explore the process of converting an existing level to World Partition.

## Using World Partition on an Existing Level

Unreal has a built-in tool which can be used to convert an existing level to use World Partition. This process can take a little bit of time, you just need to accept it is working in the background, don't panic and grab a cup of tea and a biscuit (or beverage and snack of your choice). Ideally, when building your worlds, you should determine your workload and level loading/streaming approach early in the project rather than once everything has been completed, however, this approach will work and will allow you to implement World Partition on existing levels. To use the tool the level you want to convert must be saved. If you are working on an Untitled map, it will not be available to convert. Let's give it a go:

1. From the menus, navigate to **Tools | Convert Level**.
2. This will pop up an **Asset Dialog**, this is asking you to select which level you would like to convert to use World Partition, select **WizardDesk** and click **Open**.
3. From the following pop-up, you can leave most things as standard (shown in Figure 11.4). If you want to convert your level and not keep the old one, you can enable **In Place** but we advise against that choice. Simply click **Ok.**

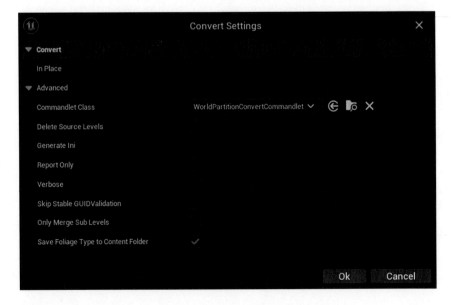

**FIGURE 11.4**    World partition convert settings dialog with default settings.

4. You will be prompted to save any unsaved assets and levels, use your judgment here.

5. You will now be greeted by a **Converting map to world partition...** dialog, which will show 0%. It will continue to show 0% for some time and then disappear. When it does, it should load the level.

6. You will notice the level has a landscape but other than that is quite empty, this is because nothing is currently loaded. In the example map, we've been using so far in the chapter, the whole map was selected as a region and loaded by default.

7. Navigate to the **World Partition** panel (if it isn't open, you can open it from **Window | World Partition | World Partition Editor**), zoom out so you can see all of the gray rectangles, these represent the various actors in the world.

8. Click and Drag around all of the actors, Right Click and select **Load Region From Selection**. You should now see everything appear!

9. There is one last thing to do, and that's to create a minimap image. To do this, navigate to **Build | Build World Partition Editor Minimap** from the menu bar. Save everything and wait for the build tool to do the job.

10. You should eventually see the minimap appear similar to Figure 11.5.

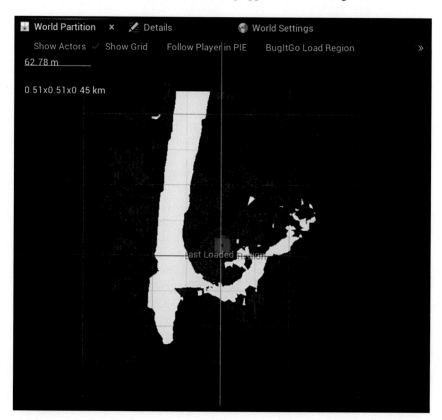

**FIGURE 11.5**   WizardDesk level minimap in the world partition editor panel.

It is worth noting that the minimap the tool generates is a static image, it will need rebuilding every time you make major revisions to the world if you plan to use it as a form of navigation in the Editor.

## Using Data Layers

Data Layers are World Partitions' approach to being able to group objects and load or unload as required when editing levels. You can approach these in a similar way that you might have used level streaming, where different levels were used for different purposes (such as a lighting level, a geometry level, a gameplay level, etc.) but instead of different levels, we place the groups on different layers. Using the newly World Partitioned Wizards Desk level, let's explore creating Data Layers and adding some objects to them:

1. Make sure you have the newly created **WizardDesk_WP** level open, if not, you should be able to find it in **Content | Maps**.
2. Navigate to **Window | World Partition | Data Layers Outliner** to open the **Data Layers** panel.
3. Right Click inside the panel and choose **Create New Data Layer**, this will create a new, **unknown** layer. This is because the layer has not been assigned to an asset.
4. Select the **unknown** layer and in the options, click the dropdown for **Data Layer Asset** and select **Data Layer** under the **CREATE NEW ASSET** section of the dropdown menu.
5. In the pop-up dialog, navigate to **Content**, Right Click and choose **New Folder**, label it *DataLayers*. Then set the name of the Data Layer Asset to *Decals*.
6. The level has already been split up, conveniently into different actor types during creation, which will make this process a lot easier as we are going to create some data layers based on object types. In the **Outliner**, select all of the actors listed in the **Decals** folder.
7. Right Click on the **Decals** data layer in the **Data Layers** panel and select **Add Selected Actors to Selected Data Layers**.
   - Alternatively, you can scroll to the bottom of the **Details** panel and expand the **Data Layers | Data Layer Assets** section and select the *Decals* data layer from the dropdown.

With the data layer setup, you can now set its initial state of being loaded and/or visible in the options in the Data Layers panel, as shown in Figure 11.6.

The checkbox in the leftmost column of the Data Layers list allows us to Toggle the Loaded In Editor flag of the Data Layer, which means if the checkbox is set to False, the actors in that data layer will not be loaded and won't be possible to view or edit in the viewport. This does not affect the loaded state of the actors when we press play to view the level in game.

**FIGURE 11.6**   The data layer outliner with data layer options.

---

### QUICK TIP

Once you've setup your Data Layers, the Data Layer panel can be docked, we recommend docking it in the same section of the Unreal Editor user interface as the Outliner.

---

## Conclusion

We have now come to the end of the chapter exploring the World Partition toolset. In this chapter, we've learned about how World Partition works and how we can change parameters to better control when objects are loaded and become visible. We've also looked at how we can make chosen actors immune to this behavior. Lastly, we've tested the World Partition conversion tool and generated a minimap for the editor. Let's check your knowledge with a quick quiz.

---

## Chapter 11  Quiz

Question 1: What is World Partition?
   a. A way of separating different regions of a map.
   b. A tool to manage the dynamic loading and unloading of regions of the world.
   c. A large wall to separate a room.

Question 2: Which of the following variable combinations controls when an object appears?
   a. Cell Size and Draw Distance.
   b. Draw Distance and Loading Range.
   c. Cell Size and Loading Range.

Question 3: How do we stop an asset from being controlled by World Partition?

    a. Give it a really big bounding box.

    b. Color it yellow.

    c. Disable Is Spatially Loaded.

    d. Set Runtime Grid to IGNORE.

Question 4: When converting a level to World Partition, which of the following are TRUE?

    a. The tool can only convert levels which are saved.

    b. When the tool is complete it will open the converted level for you.

    c. When the level opens all of the actors will be unloaded and hidden.

    d. The tool will automatically make you a minimap during the conversion process.

## Answers

Question 1: b

Question 2: c

Question 3: c

Question 4: a, b and c

# 12

## Lighting and Environment Effects

## Introduction to Lighting and Environment Effects

Lighting is an amazing topic and one that could honestly be its own unique book. In this chapter, we are going to explore some of the features within Unreal that can help us light our scene and render out an image. We'll look at the different methodologies and tools that Epic has provided to help speed up and keep our work consistent.

At the beginning of the Lighting Phase, it's important to create a Moodboard using software such as PureRef, Photoshop, MIRO or Krita. Use the Moodboard to help you hone in on how your world should look. Try to capture reference images that help you think about art fundamentals such as Color, Light and Shade, Form, Texture, Composition and Layout. Ensuring you spend enough time gathering inspirational imagery will improve the visual quality of your Unreal scenes.

## Lighting Systems and Mobility

Unreal has several lighting technologies which target different platforms. In this chapter, we'll be leveraging Unreal Engine 5's Lumen Dynamic Global Illumination and Reflection System (or Lumen for short). Our project has been configured to run with Lumen Hardware Ray Tracing at High Scalability Settings. You are most welcome to tweak the project settings should you wish to make the project run faster or run with even more advanced GPU features enabled.

### UE5 Lightmass

In addition to Lumen, there are options to create lighting for Static/Baked lighting approaches via Unreal Lightmass and Unreal GPU Lightmass. These are older systems that support lower-end platforms such as the Nintendo Switch, Xbox One and older Gaming PC's. You are likely to find developers may use a hybrid solution of different technologies.

Lighting is still one of the most expensive things a game engine can compute. For that reason, in addition to this chapter's teachings, it's worth reading up on Lightmass should you wish to target your work to game studios and lower end platforms. Epic have a horde of great documentation on their website for you to jump into, a nice place to start might be:

DOI: 10.1201/9781032663883-12

https://dev.epicgames.com/documentation/en-us/unreal-engine/lightmass-basics-in-unreal-engine?application_version=5.4

## UE5 Path Tracer

For anyone interested in pushing content toward nongaming platforms such as Arch Viz or Product Rendering, you might also want to look into Path Tracer. In comparison to Lumen, Path Tracer is not a real-time lighting solution. Path Tracer is a high-end progressive renderer that creates physically correct renders with few additional steps. We have enabled Path Tracer in the Project Settings, so you are able to try a render by changing the Lit Mode drop down in the Viewport to Path Tracer. Be warned, Path Tracer Renders can take a long time, and there are several features which are currently partially supported at the time of writing, this may mean renders look strange or require extra steps to work correctly. For an updated list, please visit Epic's Documentation here: https://dev.epicgames.com/documentation/en-us/unreal-engine/path-tracer-in-unreal-engine

## UE5 Lumen

What is Lumen? Lumen is Unreal Engine 5's solution to Global Illumination and Reflections. It is designed to work specifically for next-generation consoles (Xbox Series X and PS5) and handle very complex and large levels. Our project already has Lumen enabled, but if you are starting your own project, it is worthwhile visiting the Project Settings Menu upon setup.

The Rendering Sub Section of the Project Settings Menu has a lot of Global Illumination and Reflections Settings, here you are able to assign Methods, as shown in Figure 12.1, our project's Method is set to Lumen for both Global Illumination and

**FIGURE 12.1**   Lumen settings.

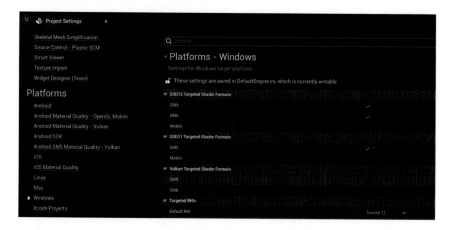

**FIGURE 12.2**  Shader model 6 and Direct X12

Reflections. There are several options available including None, Screen Space, Ray Tracing and Plugin. Try to match all the settings shown in Figure 12.1 to have a fully configured rendering setup.

In addition, you may wish to enable support for Hardware Ray Tracing. The property is also demonstrated in Figure 12.1, your computer will need a RTX/Ray Tracing Card to be able to support it. Lumen can run without Ray Tracing using a system called Distance Fields (another option you'll be asked to enable by Unreal). Working without Ray Tracing enabled will mean your imagery will look a little worse in some situations but it's still a robust approach and used commonly on several modern platforms so don't worry if your computer isn't capable of using it.

When enabling Ray Tracing and Lumen, you are quite likely to be asked to support Shader Model 6 and Direct X 12. To do this you need to match the settings shown in Figure 12.2. Here you can see SM6 is ticked and the Default RHI is set to Direct X 12. This will also allow you to support Nanite and Virtual Shadow Maps if you wish to try alternate Shadow Rendering later on.

## Unreal Light Types

When working in Levels, we can create Light by placing Light Actors. We are now going to introduce the main Light Actors types that will create most of your world's illumination.

- **Directional Light** – Directional Lights are great at emulating light sources like the sun. The light emitted features parallel rays which is great for creating the dominant light for outdoor environments. For this reason, we don't normally have more than one Directional Light in a world, though rules are always there to be broken! If you do decide to use more than one Directional Light, you may find prompts for debug warnings from other Unreal Actors, some only support one.

- **Point Light** – A Point Light behaves like a regular light bulb, emitting light in all directions. Due to the spherical casting, it is easy to accidentally cause performance issues with Point Lights. They can be used sparingly so long as they don't have too many other Point Lights.
- **Spot Light** – Spot Lights emit light in one direction, you are able to control the shape of the light with two cones. It's one of the most commonly used lights and affords a lot of customization options.
- **Rect Light** – Rect Lights behave in a similar fashion to Spot Lights aside from the light is emitted from a Rectangular Surface. They can be used for area illumination from sources such as monitors, overheads and fill lights but are generally a little more expensive to render than Spots and Point lights.
- **SkyLight** – SkyLights capture your background and apply this to the level geometry as light. You can customize the light to capture your Sky in several ways for example via an SLS Captured Scene or a SLS Specified Cubemap. SkyLights are particularly useful for raising your shadows value so they aren't pure black.

## Light Mobility

Lights have three different Mobility settings in Unreal. These are Static, Stationary and Moveable.

- **Static** – This is the fastest method for rendering, however, for our project this will be irrelevant as we are not baking lighting. Static lights are built to Lightmap textures which means they cannot be altered during runtime.
- **Stationary** – This setting affords the possibility of casting dynamic shadows but the light must remain still. You are able to manipulate the color and intensity during gameplay but not position. Unreal does not like Stationary lights to overlap, if your lights are problematic you'll see a red X near them, which indicates they are stationary and too close together.
- **Moveable** – The final light mobility is fully dynamic; we can change all properties of the light during gameplay. Nothing is baked to Lightmass, and game objects can cast shadows during run time from these lights. They are the slowest to render and what we will be using for our Lumen renders.

## Light Properties

There are many Light Properties for you to explore. We have assembled some of the common ones in a list as follows. You'll find this is just a start as you begin to use more and more of Unreal's Light Actors. If there's ever a property you are unsure about, check Epic's documentation as it's frequently updated.

- **Color** – This is the Filter color of the light, depending on the Value set, you may also increase the intensity of your light using the properties here.
- **Temperature** – An alternative to color, you can use a Kelvin Value to set the Color of your light. If you wish to do this, you need to also enable Use

Temperature. This will then override the Color value. It can be very helpful when you are trying to physically create a real-world value.

- **Intensity** – The total amount of energy a light generates.
- **Intensity Units** – Unreal affords the ability to work with Artistic and Physical Units for our lights. This is discussed in detail later on in this chapter.
- **Transform** – All lights have Location, Rotation and Scale Transforms. Placing Spotlights and Directional Lights with Pilot Mode (CTRL + SHIFT + P) is a great way to target a light to look at a particular location. Scaling a light has a knock-on implication with lighting, you'll find that the Attenuation Radius will alter as you scale a light up or down.
- **Attenuation Radius** – This is the light's influence. Not all lights have this property, you can utilize it on Points, Spots and Rect Lights to control falloff.
- **Channels** – Lights can illuminate actors on three specific channels (0, 1 and 2). You can think of these as layers. Using Channels, you are able to illuminate specific meshes or parts of a world by setting lights and other actors to specific channels. This is helpful when you don't want to illuminate a particular part of a level and target one precise mesh.
- **Functions** – A light function is a Material that alters a light's intensity. These can be used to great effect to apply bespoke textural details or animation such as light flickering.
- **IES Profiles** – Illuminating Engineering Society (IES) has a specific file format which we can use in Unreal. The format helps to describe brightness and fall of a light based on real-world counterparts. IES profiles can be applied to Points, Spots and Rectangular Lights. Any of the above Light types can load in an IES Texture to see the effect. To acquire Light Profiles, it's worth visiting Bulb Manufacturer websites and IES Profile libraries as well as the FAB Marketplace.
- **Cast Shadows** – Lights have many shadowing options, by default, in the later activities in this chapter, we shall be using Cast Dynamic Shadows with Ray Tracing applied. This grants us a very high-quality shadow. Where performance is a factor, you may need to downgrade shadows to other systems such as Virtual Shadow Maps or Cascade Shadowing.
- **Indirect Lighting Intensity** – This value represents how much the light contributes to the Global Illumination of the Scene. A higher value will mean the light has a stronger intensity in the Lumen GI.
- **Volumetric Scattering Intensity** – This property allows us to control how much intensity a light should have when using Fog Actors. We can exaggerate certain lights to make their light shafts/volumetric effects more present. We can also disable Volumetric Scattering where we might want a fill light that doesn't get shown as a bright, foggy bulb.
- **Inverse Square Falloff** – Attenuation and Falloff are calculated by the Inverse Square Falloff rule by default. We can disable this if we wish to work with less realistic light and gain some performance. In most instances, though this will be left on.

- **Cone Angles** – Some actors such as Spots and Rectangles have multiple cone properties to allow us to control the shape of a light and its falloff. Toggling out of Game View (G on your Keyboard) will allow you to see a light's primitive cone shape.

## Physical versus Artistic Units

The Unreal Lighting system has several options for Lighting Units and Lighting variables. It's important to know what they are and how they interact with the tools in the engine. There is quite a large variation in the way that studios and artists interact with the tools. You are likely to find that some developers will adopt a Physically Defined workflow, whereas others may prefer to work with Artistic Units. In both instances, it's important to be flexible and adapt to what's needed for the job. To further complicate the matter, lighting is often a major area for optimization as it can have a significant hit on performance. You'll therefore see studios create very precise budgets for lighting workflow and decisions.

What are the options for lighting units? When working with Point, Spot and Rectangular lights artists can swap between:

- **Candela** (CD) – One Candela is roughly the same brightness as one candle. In Unreal, it's a measurement of light/luminous intensity emitted across a solid angle of one steradian. A steradian is the area of a sphere which is equal to the square of the sphere's radius. You can imagine the result of the calculation as a cone shape.
- **Lumen** (LM) – Like Candela, Lumen is a physical lighting unit which means we can research real-world bulbs and enter their Lumen value in Unreal. In comparison to Candela, Lumen represents the perceived/total power of a light.
- **Unitless** – This is an Unreal-specific value system that is not physically based but links back to older versions of Unreal Engine 4. Its value ranges can be many thousands in comparison and is more artistically driven than the others. However, we can somewhat convert to a Candela equivalent as Epic has stated that One Candela is approximately 625 Unitless Units.

For Directional Lights, which are often the sun/main light source in our Levels, the units are measured in Lux. Again, this is a Physical Value, which you can research and compare against photographers and movie directors to have parity in your values. However, out of the box, Unreal's Directional Lighting system works with a very low Lux value of around 10 for daylight. If you apply a Physically Correct Midday lux of around 120000 you will see that your viewport becomes bright white, this will be due to the Exposure and Camera setup which we shall look at later.

Unreal also has the option to control physically based falloff. In the light settings, there is a property called Inverse Square Falloff, this is always enabled by default. We can disable it if we wish to gain some performance or perhaps create a very consistent fill light.

Unreal handles the conversion between lighting units automatically. If you would like to explore how this is done you can review the documentation following this link.

https://dev.epicgames.com/documentation/en-us/unreal-engine/using-physical-lighting-units-in-unreal-engine?application_version=5.3

## Environment Light Mixer

What's the best place to start if we just want to render an outdoor Scene? Epic has recently integrated a new Menu/Toolset called the Environment Light Mixer. This tool can quickly create the necessary Actors to help control the illumination of outdoor scenes. The tool can work with existing light setups and also empty levels.

To help us through the early stages of world building such as Landscape sculpting, foliage placement and material generation, it's wise to have some temporary lights in the scene so we can see what we are making. However, once we reach the lighting stage these actors are often disabled or deleted so that we can begin lighting from scratch. There is an alternative to this in bigger teams where you might be tasked to light a small section of a level and another artist tackles the larger mood of the level. Should this be the case, it's just a matter of communicating responsibilities and workflows to ensure things go well.

You can launch the Environment Light Mixer from the Windows Menu. Once opened it will give you a shortcut to the Main Environmental Light Actors. These actors are listed as follows.

- Directional Light
- Sky Atmosphere
- Volumetric Cloud
- Exponential Height Fog
- Sky Light

If your Level already has the above Actors in situ the Menu will showcase "Minimal" properties by default. You may expand what information the tool showcases by changing the Minimal Dropdown to Normal/Advanced. If no properties are shown, then it may be the case your world lacks the Actors and they need creating. You will be able to tell this is the case as the UI will feature a Create Button for any missing Environmental Light Actor.

The palette is helpful as it keeps a lot of the main options in one place. However, you may find that you do not use it. It's purely there to try and keep the sheer amount of lighting options in one place. If you prefer to hop between the Actors using the World Outliner and Details Panel that is also absolutely fine.

## Post Processing

Unreal has a very flexible and powerful actor called the Post Processing Volume. This actor can be utilized to apply a variety of effects to the player's Camera. There are a couple of ways in which the Post Process Volume can be used.

1. As a temporary effect that occurs when a player or camera reaches a certain point in a level. For example, when a player reaches a lava pit the screen might tint red or additional heat haze might be applied.
2. As a holistic effect that applies to the players'/viewers' camera at all times. The layer can be used for applying consistent visual styling such as exposure, bloom, grading, vignettes and much more.

As world builders, we need to use the Post Processing Volume in all projects to help control our visual fidelity. In most situations, we will be using these Actors to apply a series of visual effects to the screen in one go. This actor can take a long time to master, there are many hundreds of properties to go through. Try not to be intimidated and experiment with the actor and your worlds.

We'll look at a couple of workflows and important parameters to change in most projects; however, you will certainly need to experiment with the actor outside of the book's exercises. We'll start by exploring some of the key aspects of the Post Process Volume and how we might leverage them in our level.

Post Processing supports many effects, some of the common ones to begin with are:

- **Exposure** – This affects how light changes based on our level's luminance. It attempts to recreate how our eyes adjust to changing lighting settings. For example, moving from a dimly lit cave to a bright meadow. We can leverage Exposure to match real-world lighting and values from photography when working on physically accurate scenes.

- **Bloom** – helps to create the feathering of light extending from a bright area of an image. Sometimes also called a Halo Bloom, it attempts to replicate cameras being overwhelmed by very bright lighting. In Unreal, we have two options: Standard and Convolution. The Standard Bloom is more performant for games, whereas Convolution tends to look nicer and better replicate the physical effect. For world building projects and portfolio renders, try using the Convolution Bloom and begin by adjusting its intensity. You can also add in textures for the Convolution effect to further detail the result. It can be quite easy to over power your renders so small adjustments are wise when adjusting intensities.

- **Lens Flares** – These occur as very bright light scatters through glass. In Unreal, we have a variety of properties to control the effect including BokehSize, BokehShape, Tint, as well the Overall Intensity. They can be extremely distracting so need to be used with subtlety and caution.

- **Dirt Masks** – Dirt Masks are textures that replicate the effect of dirt, dust and/or grime that is sitting on top of a camera lens. It's a very noticeable effect and won't fit all styles such as clean or very stylized worlds, but it adds a layer of grit and grime when you need to make more battletorn scenes. We are able to control the Dirt via a Texture, its intensity and tint.

- **Chromatic Aberration** – This often occurs when there is a large contrast in a traditional image. The effect distorts edges of meshes and objects adding a fringe of color. In Unreal, we can control when this starts to happen via an offset and also how intense it is. Like some of the other effects discussed in this section, gently is the way forward. It's very easy to end up with lots of green and red outlines around meshes accidently.

- **Vignette** – This applies a darkening to the corners of our image. We can raise the intensity to bring the viewers' attention to the middle of an image almost as if they are looking through a keyhole. Unlike other DCCs, Unreal's Vignette only applies a darkening tint and does not offer the ability to add a white/brightening tint.

- **Color Grading** – Unreal has many options to control your world's color, contrast, saturation and many other filmic values. The Post Process Volume has several distinct rollouts with lots of options to get stuck into. Color spaces vary and can be quite complex; it is worth referring to Unreal Documentation for a complete breakdown if you need to export renders to work on in other DCCs. Some artist pipelines prefer to complete Color Grading in other DCCs such as Photoshop, Nuke and or DaVinci Resolve.

- **Motion Blur** – This blurs and streaks fast-moving actors in Unreal. We can control options such as the Amount, Max, Per Object Size and Target FPS of the blur. Depending on what you have in your world, you may not require this feature. Should your world have many fast-moving objects you may wish to add some subtle blur or even extreme amounts if you are planning high-speed chases!

- **Film Grain** – Replicates the visual appearance of film. It adds random noise/particles to the frames to create a film-like style. We can manipulate the type of Film Grain texture, the intensity and many other properties to dial in our desired look.

- **Global Illumination** – A system that controls light bouncing in a level from light sources (direct lighting) to create indirect illumination. This adds an extra layer of realism and complexity to our worlds. The Post Process Volume affords us many options, we can select a type of Global Illumination such as None, Lumen, Screen Space and Ray Tracing. In the book's project, we have elected to use Lumen, by all means, explore the other options. The Post Process allows us to increase the amount of detail, quality and options like Lumen distance, which will all improve your Lumen Global Illumination at the cost of performance.

- **Reflections** – We can select from several methods for reflections. These are Lumen, Screen Space and Ray tracing. Lumen reflections are very good particularly with ray tracing enabled, Screen Space reflections are performant but have a lower quality and Ray Traced reflections are an older high-quality approach which is likely to be removed at some point in the future and become depreciated. As world builders, we can mix and match Global Illumination (GI) and reflections methods for example Lumen GI and Screen Space Reflections. This is what some developers might refer to as Hybrid rendering and it is done to maintain a certain quality level at high speed. In the provided project we have set the reflections to Lumen. You are able to increase the quality substantially in the Post Process by adding extra bounces and enabling High-Quality Reflections. Increasing each of these settings will decrease FPS.

- **Translucency** – Affords control over how surfaces such as Glass and Water are rendered. Anything that is see through and has an opacity material. By default, Translucency will be set to the Raster method. Raster is the fastest approach, however, when changing to Ray Tracing you will see a noticeable improvement in visual quality and complexity. There are multiple options to further improve the effect, such as increasing samples, refraction and shadow types. The Post Process is extremely flexible to afford developers the option to turn on and off features as needed.

This section introduced some of the many options in the Post Process, it really is a great place to test drive and customize your Unreal imagery. We'll now explore Unreal's Lighting System and Post Processing by putting them into use in a couple of exercises.

## Lighting Exercise One: Let There Be DayLight

We've provided several quick start Lighting maps which showcase the final world illuminated in a couple of different ways. These include Midday, Golden Hour and Nighttime. The nighttime scene also includes an illuminated interior from our first book with more goodies to explore, enjoy! We are now going to start a global lighting pass using an example level. The goal here is to establish something similar to a cloudy midday scene. Let's Get Started!

### Lighting a Cloudy Midday Exterior

1. Open the **Landscape_Lighting_Start** level which can be found in the **Content | Maps** folder. The map should look like the example shown in Figure 12.3.
2. Open the Environment Light Mixer by navigating to **Window | Env. Light Mixer**.
3. Click the **Create…** buttons for each of the five actors available in the **Env. Light Mixer**, these are **Sky Light**, **Atmospheric Light**, **Sky Atmosphere**, **Volumetric Cloud** and **Height Fog**. These buttons can be seen in Figure 12.4.

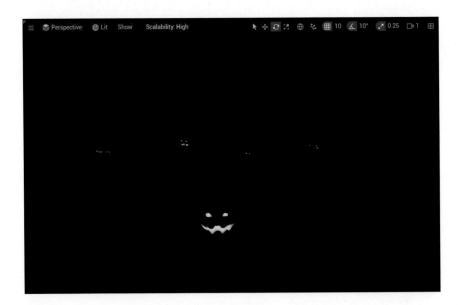

**FIGURE 12.3** Lighting start map.

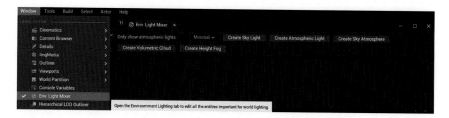

**FIGURE 12.4** Environment light mixer.

4. Make a new Folder in the **World Outliner** called *Lighting*. Place this folder inside the existing **A_Post&Light** Folder.

5. Add the five created Actors to this folder. These are **DirectionalLight, ExponentialHeightFog, SkyAtmosphere, SkyLight** and **VolumetricCloud**. Note that the actors are called different things initially in the **Environment Light Mixer**.

6. *Optional Task.*

---

**OPTIONAL STEP**

Using the Window | Levels Menu, Create a new Sub Level called MiddayLighting. Move the five newly created Actors to this new lighting level and Save. This step is not necessary for this exercise, but you may find it useful having a separate lighting level will allow you to test out different times of day much easier. For example, you could have a lighting level for Midday, Dusk, Sunset, etc.

---

7. With all of our Environment Light Mixer Actors created and set up, the **Env. Light Mixer** panel will show a lot more properties like those shown in Figure 12.5. In addition, Figure 12.6 showcases the default appearance of the environment with the actors created.

8. Using the **Place Actors** menu, navigate to the Visual Effects Tab and add a **Post Process Volume** to the world. It doesn't matter where this volume exists in space for now. Select the **PostProcessVolume** in the **World Outliner** and search for the property **Infinite Extend/Unbound** and enable it. This will apply the settings in the Volume to the screen no matter where we are in the Level. You can see a Post Process Volume in the world in Figure 12.7.

9. With the **PostProcessVolume** selected, search for **Max Brightness** and **Min Brightness** and set these to *1*. This locks the Exposure Value, which stops the eye adaption. It will also now lock the level to quite a low Exposure Value which means we will not be using Physically Correct units for this exercise. You can review these settings against the example in Figure 12.8.

10. Select the **DirectionalLight** and try to aim the light so there are some interesting contact shadows hitting the main building. Figure 12.9 shows shadows being cast on the wall from the main windows, for example. You may find it easier to angle the Directional Light using **Pilot** mode, to try

**FIGURE 12.5**   Environment light mixer properties.

**FIGURE 12.6**   Default scene appearance.

**FIGURE 12.7**   Post process volume.

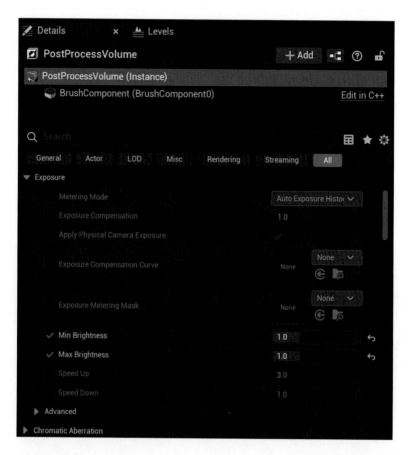

**FIGURE 12.8** Exposure values.

**FIGURE 12.9** Directional light angle.

this, you need to select the Directional Light and then hit the shortcut CTRL+SHIFT+P. When finished, remember to Eject/Stop Piloting, you will see a **Stop** button in the upper left of the active viewport. You should notice the Atmosphere reacts correctly to the pitch of the Directional Light, the steeper the angle the closer to midday the lighting will feel while if the angle gets close to the horizon the coloration and shadows will move into a more sunrise or sunset feel.

11. Select the **DirectionalLight** again, search for the property *Cast* and then enable **Cast Ray Traced Shadows**. If these shadows are a bit too sharp for your taste you can soften them by raising the **Source Angle** to a value of your choice.

12. Experiment with enabling **Cast Shadows on Clouds, Cast Shadows on Atmosphere** and **Cast Cloud Shadows**.

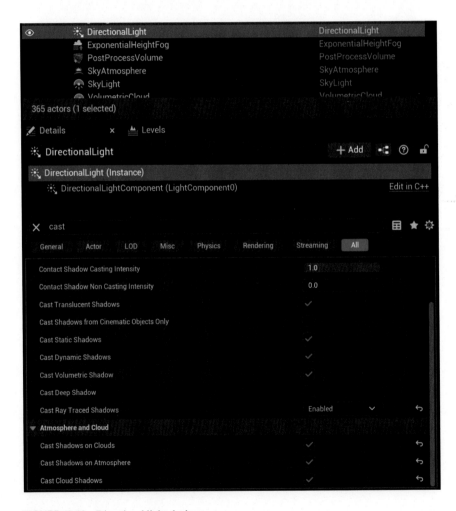

**FIGURE 12.10**   Directional light shadows.

**FIGURE 12.11** Volumetric fog.

13. By enabling **Cast Cloud Shadows**, you'll notice that the intensity of the image will drop as the world becomes more overcast. You can counter this a bit by raising the Directional Light's **Intensity** up to *25*.

14. Next, select the **ExponentialHeightFog** Actor, this adds some distance fog to the world. We can make it behave physically correct by enabling the **Volumetric Fog** Boolean.

15. Adjust the **Start Distance** to *2500*, this pushes the fog effect away from the camera. Finally, adjust the **Albedo** to be a light blue color and set **Fog Density** to be *0.1*. Figure 12.11 shows the key settings, for this exercise, do not thicken the effect too much as we are going for a Midday setting with some light cloud.

16. Figures 12.12 and 12.13 showcase some minor tweaks to the scene by adding some Post Process Effects. In Figure 12.12, we can add a little bit of **Vignette** (darkening to the edges of the viewport). I'd suggest keeping this quite minor until the end, a value of around *0.5* will work for now. In Figure 12.13, changing the **Bloom Method** to *Convolution* will continue to help make things look more realistic overall. You won't see a dramatic change at this point as we don't have many strong light sources aside from the Key Directional Light.

17. Another fun Post Process effect is shown in Figure 12.14 which is the **Dirt Mask**. To try this, enable the **Dirt Mask Texture** and search for the texture *T_ScreenDirt02_w*, if you can't find it, ensure that you have **Show Engine Content** enabled in the **Settings** of the **Content Browser**. Next, raise the **Dirt Mask Intensity** to around *100*. You should now see several lens imperfections appear on the screen.

**FIGURE 12.12**   Post process vignette.

**FIGURE 12.13**   Post process bloom.

18. Another one of the Environment Light Mixer Actors was the Volumetric Cloud. Figure 12.15 shows adjusted parameters in the Details Panel, denoted by the Reset to Default arrow, these changes add a little more complexity to clouds appearance.

At this point, we've created our main Actors and illuminated our world to roughly Midday using artistic values. You could experiment with the Color Temperature

**FIGURE 12.14** Dirt mask.

**FIGURE 12.15** Volumetric cloud.

of the Directional Light by enabling Use Temperature and then setting the Temperature value. Daylight is approximately 5600k and values above 6500k start to get more overcast. If you prefer you can always adjust the Light Color instead of the temperature.

When you are happy with any adjustments and are ready to move on, navigate to File | Save Current Level As... to save the map, name it *Landscape_Lighting_MiddayArtistic_YourName*.

## Lighting Exercises Two: Golden Hour

We'll now explore a similar workflow but using more real-world values. You'll now see much larger values being used, while this may be a little confusing or strange at first, it's important to note that using real-world values helps align what we are doing with other fields such as Photography. Let's get cracking!

1. Open the **Landscape_Lighting_Start** level which can be found in the **Content | Maps** folder.
2. Navigate to **Window | Env. Light Mixer** to open the Environment Light Mixer panel.
3. Click the **Create** buttons for the five actors available in the **Env. Light Mixer**, these are; **Sky Light, Atmospheric Light, Sky Atmosphere, Volumetric Cloud** and **Height Fog**.
4. Make a new Folder in the **World Outliner**, called **Lighting**. Place this folder inside the existing **A_Post&Light** Folder.
5. Add the five created Actors to this folder. These are **DirectionalLight, ExponentialHeightFog, SkyAtmosphere, SkyLight** and **VolumetricCloud**. Note that, the actors are called different things initially in the Environment Light Mixer.
6. Navigate to **File | Save Current Level As...** to save the map, name it *Landscape_Lighting_GoldenHour*.
7. Using the **Place Actors** menu, navigate to the Visual Effects Tab and add a **PostProcessVolume** to the world. It doesn't matter where this volume exists in space for now. Select the **PostProcessVolume** in the **World Outliner** and find the property **Infinite Extend/Unbound** and *enable it*. This will apply the settings in the Volume to the screen no matter where we are in the Level.
8. Select the **DirectionalLight**, set its **Y Rotation** to *1* and its **Z Rotation** to *-285* using the **Details** panel.
9. Next, set the **Directional Lights Intensity** to *10000 lux*. Enable **Ray Traced Shadows, Cast Shadows on Clouds, Cast Shadows on Atmosphere** and **Cast Cloud Shadows**. You will most likely see the screen go quite bright due to the large intensity on the **DirectionalLight**.
10. Select the **PostProcessVolume**, expand the **Exposure** rollout and change the **Metering Mode** to *Manual*. Let's explore a bit of theory before moving on.

With the Exposure Control set to Manual, we are now going to explore the Camera Exposure Controls within the Post Process. These controls are great if you are looking to match physically based properties and want to share experience with photography. It is not a required part of the workflow, however, as some studios will not utilize these properties but be aware, some will.

So, what do we have to play with?

- **Shutter Speed** – this is the camera's shutter speed measured in seconds. A faster/shorter shutter speed will lead to a quicker exposure and let in less light, whereas a slower shutter speed will lead to a larger exposure and let in a lot more light. We usually calculate Shutter speed as 1/X, which returns Shutter speed in fractions of a second. The larger the X value often the more useful the setting is for capturing fast movement. Both quick and slow shutter speeds can be useful for adding blur. In our scene today, there isn't too much movement so values from a couple of seconds to perhaps 1/25 are useful.

- **ISO** – This controls the amount of light/sensitivity of light a camera has. Lower values of 100 are useful when there is more light, for example, mid-day, whereas nighttime lighting requires a larger ISO perhaps 1600. In addition, if your camera moves a lot in Unreal, it can be helpful to try a combination of larger ISO and fast shutter speed.

- **Aperture** – This controls the camera's lens. A lower value will lead to greater blurring of objects in the foreground and background that are not in the focal region. It will also let in more light. A higher value will reduce blurring but let in less light.

- **Maximum Aperture** – This sets the largest opening of the camera lens and provides a ceiling for the Aperture value.

- **Number of diaphragm blades** – This controls the shape of the Bokeh. Generally, lower values will make any Bokeh more rectangular, whilst higher values will produce a rounder Bokeh.

The above values are great for setting up the overall Exposure for the viewport, but if you render using Unreal Camera Actors, you will experience some differences in appearance. This is because Unreal's Camera Actors have a property called Post Process Blend Weight. If the Blend Weight is left at the default value of 1 Camera Actor settings will override Post Process Volume settings. It's important to go through each Cinematic Camera's Filmback and Lens settings to ensure they match what you'd like to achieve with a shot. This is not a bug, cameras are set up to offer you greater freedom and precision, just as in real life, you might have a box of different lens' you use on the same day.

Let's get back to our scene!

1. Select the **PostProcessVolume**, open the **Camera** Settings. Set the **Shutter Speed** value to *25* and set the **ISO** to *700*. This should now bring the scene back into Exposure.

2. The scene is currently lacking a bit of punch which we can get back by select-ing the **VolumetricCloud** Actor. Then we need to enable **Use Per Sample Atmospheric Light Transmittance**. You should see a much-improved col-oration of the clouds.

3. If the scene still feels a little dark, try selecting the **SkyLight** Actor and rais-ing the **Intensity Scale**.

4. The Golden Hour light is really nice and also offers the opportunity for some light shafts. Select the **DirectionalLight** and *enable* both **Light Shaft Occlusion** and also **Light Shaft Bloom**. If you move the Viewport Camera opposing the sun, you should now see some Light Shafts streak across the Landscape, as shown in Figure 12.16.

**FIGURE 12.16**   Light shafts.

5. When you are ready use **File | Save Current Level As** to save the map as *Landscape_Lighting_GoldenHour_YourName*.

**USEFUL TIP**

If you use real-world light values, many of your glowing materials will need to scale up to be seen. You can achieve this easily by dividing your current emissive input with an Eye Adaptation node in the Material Editor.

## Lighting Exercises Three: Nighttime

We are now going to try lighting an evening scene. This will expose you to working with artistic units and some mesh manipulation as well as some of the other workflows we've followed so far. This time we will use a Sky Sphere, which was used to set up many skies in Unreal Engine 4. This Sky Sphere is great when used for evening lighting and starry skies. Let's get started!

1. Open the **Landscape_Lighting_Start** level, which can be found in the **Content | Maps** folder.
2. Navigate to **Window | Env. Light Mixer** to open the Environment Light Mixer.
3. Click the **Create** buttons for the five actors available in the **Env. Light Mixer**, these are **Sky Light**, **Atmospheric Light**, **Sky Atmosphere**, **Volumetric Cloud** and **Height Fog**.

4. Navigate to the **Place Actors** menu and add a **BP_Sky_Sphere** to the level.

5. Using the **Place Actors** menu, navigate to the Visual Effects Tab and add a **Post Process Volume** to the World. It doesn't matter where this volume exists in space for now. Select the **Post Process Volume** in the **World Outliner** and search for the property **Infinite Extend/Unbound** and enable it. Then Search for the properties **Min Brightness** and **Max Brightness** and set them both to *1*.

6. Make a new Folder in the **World Outliner**, called *Lighting*. Place this folder inside the existing **A_Post&Light** Folder.

7. Add the seven created Actors to this folder. These are **DirectionalLight**, **ExponentialHeightFog**, **SkyAtmosphere**, **SkyLight**, **VolumetricCloud**, **BP_Sky_Sphere** and **PostProcessVolume**.

8. Select the **DirectionalLight** Actor. Set the **Intensity** to a value of *6*. Set the **Light Color** Value to be, **R**=*0.19*, **G**=*0.22* and **B**=*0.59*. Then set the **Source Soft Angle** to *1.42* which will soften the shadows. Now enable **Transmission**, this will allow light to scatter through Subsurface Materials such as foliage, curtains and candles. Lastly, enable **Ray-Traced Shadows**.

9. With the Directional Light setup, use Pilot mode or the Transform commands to angle the light however you wish. In the provided example, we pointed the light to the open windows of the building to afford light to filter through the curtains.

10. Now select the **BP_Sky_Sphere** Actor. There are quite a lot of properties to adjust, let's get started. *Disable* the value **Colors Determined By Sun Position**. Set both **Cloud Speed** and **Cloud Opacity** to *0*, we have already added the **Volumetric Clouds** actor to render our clouds. Increase the **Star Brightness** to *12*. Set the **Sun Height** to –*0.4 and* set the **Horizon Falloff** to *2.5*. Now we need to pick some colors, set the **Zenith Color** to either black or a very dark blue. Set the **Horizon Color** to a very dark gray. Lastly, set the **Overall Color** to a mid gray this will reduce the visibility of the stars.

11. Select the **Exponential Height Fog** using the **World Outliner**. Raise the **Fog Density** to *0.8*. Next, raise the **Fog Height Falloff** to *2*, this will allow us to see the sky but keep the fog dense near the ground. *Enable* **Volumetric Fog** and raise the **Start Distance** to around *1024*. Change the **Albedo** of the Fog to a dark gray. Then lower the **Extinction Scale** to *0.75*.

12. Next, select the **VolumetricCloud** Actor. Set the **View Sample Count Scale** to *8*, the **Shadow Tracing Distance** to *50*, and the **Stop Tracing Transmittance Threshold** to *0.15*. you should now see further contrast in the clouds.

13. Let's now select the **SkyLight** Actor. First disable **Real Time Capture**. Unlike our other Levels, we are going to use a texture in combination with our Skylight. To do this, set the **Source Type** to *SLS Specified Cubemap*. Set the **Cubemap Texture** to *Kiara_1_dawn_4k*. Set the **Source Cubemap Angle** to *330*. Set the **Intensity Scale** to *0*. Change the **Light Color** to a Sky Blue. You can also disable **Cast Shadows** to make the light a bit more performant.

**FIGURE 12.17**    Nighttime base.

14. We finally need to set up our **SkyAtmosphere**. Select the **SkyAtmosphere** Actor and adjust the following settings.
    - Set **Rayleigh Scattering Scale** to *0.15*.
    - Set the **Rayleigh Scattering Color** to a very Dark Grey.
    - Set **Rayleigh Exponential Distribution** to *4*.
    - Increase the **Height Fog Contribution** to *2*.
    - Set the **Aerial Perspective View Distance Scale** to *2*.

We've now set up our base for the nighttime scene. The Environment Light Mixer Actors shown in Figure 12.17 do very little to make anything pop in the scene or draw attention. The basic scene lights while extremely powerful will not always do the job for you, they are often just the start of a big process. We are now going to look at how we can reinforce some interesting details in the scene with extra actors and lights to make things fun.

1. Using the **Place Actors** menu, try placing Two **Point Lights** inside the meshes **OutsideLantern0_Mesh** and **OutsideLantern1_Mesh**, which you can locate using the **World Outliner**. Label these lights something sensible such as *OutdoorLanternPointLight1* and *OutdoorLanternPointLight2* and place them both in a folder called Lights in the **World Outliner**.

2. Select both **OutdoorLanternPointLights** and adjust their properties as follows. Make sure both lights **Mobility** is set to *Moveable*. Enable use **Temperature** and set the value to be *3000k*. Change their **Attenuation Radius** to *300* and set their **Intensity** to be *3 Candelas*. Enable the

**Transmission** value which will make the light color richer. Disable **Cast Ray Traced Shadows** and enable **Distance Field Shadows**. The results can be seen in Figure 12.18.

In addition to the Point Lights, we can also use Spot Lights. In Figure 12.19, a Spot Light actor has been added to pick out the front of the building. Let's try this next!

**FIGURE 12.18** Outdoor point lights.

**FIGURE 12.19** Building fills and keys.

1. Using the **Place Actor** Menu, add a **Spotlight** to the level.
2. Place the light in the **Lights** folder and label it *BuildingSpotLight*.
3. Angle the light to catch the entrance side of the building shown in Figure 12.19.
4. Set the **Intensity** to *250 Candelas*.
5. Set the **Light Color** to a very light blue.
6. Increase the **Attenuation Radius** to *20000* units and set the **Cone Angle** to *80*.

This light should now subtly pick out the building as if it was being illuminated by the moon. We have to be careful adding too many sources that look like Directional Lights, in this example, it's believable as there's no moon in the sky to break the illusion.

Another cool addition we can use at nighttime is localized fog. In Epic's Content Examples, they showcase the use of fog Blueprints that can be placed around the scene.

1. In the **Content Browser**, navigate to **Content | Blueprints**.
2. Drag and Drop a **GroundFogBlueprint** into the level. In Figure 12.20, you can see one of these Blueprints has been added to the world.

Fog Actors can be added across several parts of the World, it doesn't just have to be a large plane in the distance. In Figure 12.21, several GroundFogSheet Blueprints have been added going up the hill to help bring attention to the building. Figure 12.22 shows the result of the Blueprints with the actors deselected. The Details Panel provides the option to tint the Actor's Color and make them glow a little, in the example, the Actors have a subtle turquoise hue to stand out.

**FIGURE 12.20**   Fog sheets.

**FIGURE 12.21** Fog sheets part 2.

**FIGURE 12.22** Fog sheets rendered.

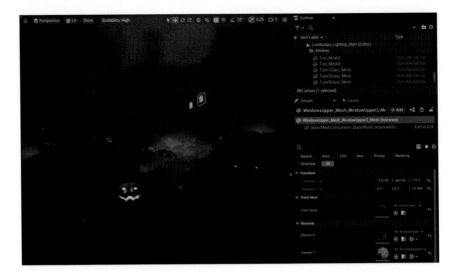

**FIGURE 12.23**   Swapping window materials.

In some worlds, a simple trick might be to simply swap a mesh or a material when lighting conditions change. In Figure 12.23, we demonstrate this by swapping out the windows of the building. The additional glow now adds a strong attention grabber to the building. Simple changes like this are nice as it can add a lot with just a texture alteration. To do this:

1. Select the **WindowsUpper_Mesh_WindowUpper3_Mesh**.
2. Change the **Element 1** material to *CI_WindowUpperEmissive*.
3. Repeat the first two steps for the other upper floor windows.

As soon as you start adding more light sources and brighter sources you might wish to swap in the Convolution Bloom method shown in Figure 12.24. This method can give you some nicer Bloom shapes. To do this:

1. Select the **PostProcessVolume** from the **World Outliner**.
2. Locate the **Method** setting in the **Lens | Bloom** section and change it to *Convolution*.

Our final step for our nighttime scene is the addition of time-of-day VFX. In Figure 12.25, a Niagara Fire Flies system has been added several times up the hill. This effect works a bit like the fog in that it draws the viewer's eye up the hill and adds additional brightness around key and fun parts of the world. To do this:

1. In the Content Browser, navigate to **Content | VFX**.
2. Drag and Drop a **FireFlies_System** asset into the world.

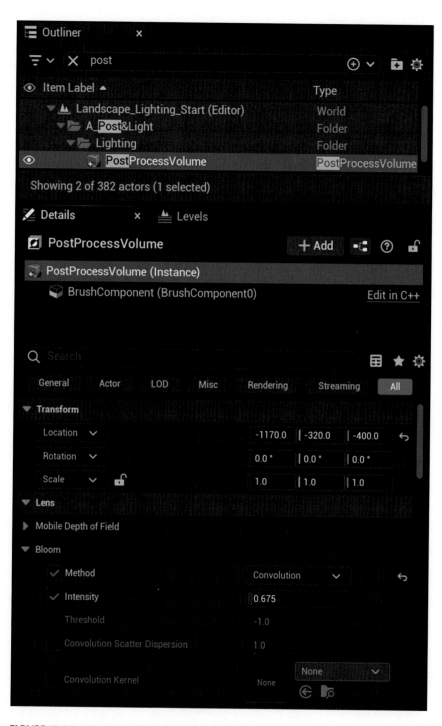

**FIGURE 12.24** Convolution bloom settings.

**FIGURE 12.25**   Lighting with VFX fire flies.

We've now explored several key ways of adding additional light, detail and contrast to our nighttime world. We shall now move onto different ways of generating imagery from Unreal to help showcase our efforts and World Building work.

## Screenshots and Capturing Your Work

There are three main ways you can export imagery from Unreal. The options are Console Commands, High Resolution Screenshot Tool, and) MovieRender Cue/ Sequencer. Each option adds more time than the previous one, console commands being the fastest to use and Movie Render Cue or Sequencer being the slowest. There isn't a right or wrong way as such to capture imagery from Unreal. We'll explore a couple of scenarios and considerations for exporting images.

When exporting any imagery, it's wise to start from a Cinematic Camera Actor. Having a Cinematic Camera Actor will ensure you have locked in any compositional and framing choices. Figure 12.26 shows how the Perspective View has been swapped to the Camera OutsideFullMagicStopView by clicking on the Perspective text in the Viewport.

Let's explore how we might capture this camera using Console Commands. To replicate the steps please follow these steps.

1. Open the **Landscape_Lighting_Nighttime** level.
2. Change to the Camera **OutsideFullMagicStopView** by clicking the **Perspective** text in the Viewport and searching the **Placed Cameras** list.
3. Press the Tilde Key (~) to Open the **Console**.
4. Type *HighResShot 2*.

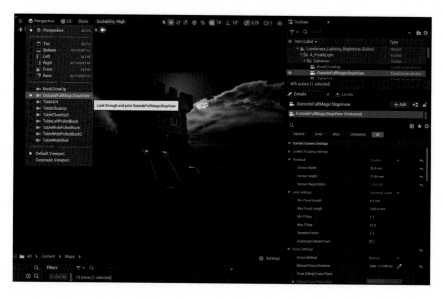

**FIGURE 12.26**   Cinematic camera setup.

5. Locate your Projects folder and inside it navigate to the directory **Saved | Screenshots | WindowsEditor**.
6. You should then see your screenshot.

By using the command HighResShot 2, we have captured a screenshot that is double the active viewport. But what happens if we want a specific resolution? You could repeat the above swapping out the command with the following

HighResShot 1920x1080

The screen resolution can be increased as needed, for example, an 8k command would be

HighResShot 7680x4320

Let's now try the **High Resolution Screenshot Tool**, let's switch cameras to keep things interesting. Please follow these instructions:

1. Open the **Landscape_Lighting_Nighttime** level.
2. Change to the Camera **TableCloseUp** by clicking the **Perspective** text in the Viewport and searching the **Placed Cameras** list.
3. Click the three horizontal lines button which is the top left icon in the Viewport.
4. From the drop-down menu, select **High Resolution Screenshot**.
5. You should now see the **High Resolution Screenshot** Tool as seen in Figure 12.27.
6. You now have many options to experiment with before clicking the **Capture** button.

**FIGURE 12.27**　High Resolution Screenshot Tool.

The tool affords options such as Timestamps, Depth Masks and Buffer Visualizations. This gives you the ability to save more complex imagery out of the engine for further processing in other DCCs. You can achieve the same functionality with the console command, however, it requires you to remember a lot of text, whereas the visual UI is simple. Epic provides a full breakdown of console command possibilities here if you'd like to explore more.

https://dev.epicgames.com/documentation/en-us/unreal-engine/taking-screenshots-in-unreal-engine?application_version=5.3

In our final test, let's experiment with using Movie Render Cue to quickly export a level's Cameras. In the provided project, Movie Render Cue has already been enabled, but in your custom project work you will need to enable it via the Plugins Menu. Let's begin!

1. Open the **Landscape_Lighting_Nighttime** level.
2. Local the EditorUtilityWidget **StillRenderSetupAutomation**, you can find this within the directory shown in Figure 12.28. You will need to enable both **Show Engine Content** and **Show Plugin Content** by clicking the **Settings** button in a **Content Browser**.
3. **Right Click** on the **StillRenderSetupAutomation** Widget and select **Run Editor Utility Widget**. You should see the menu shown in Figure 12.29.
4. From the menu, you can set the **Resolution, Output Folder** and **Settings Preset** to Apply.
5. It's worth exploring the **Settings Present** in your own time as there are a vast amount of options here.
6. Then you can select between **Create Sequencer for Selected**, which will create a sequence for just one camera or **Create Sequence for All Cameras**, which will create a sequence for all cameras in your world.
7. Select **Create Sequence for All Cameras** when you are ready.
8. Navigate to **Window | Cinematic | Movie Render Cue** to open **Movie Render Cue**.
9. You'll then see a list of Cameras as per Figure 12.30.

**FIGURE 12.28** StillRenderSetupAutomation content browser.

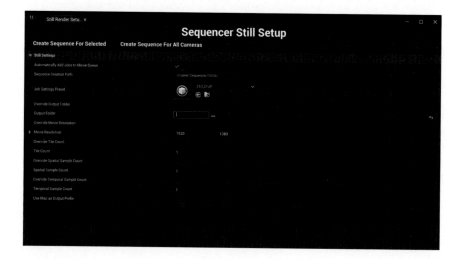

**FIGURE 12.29** StillRenderSetupAutomation widget.

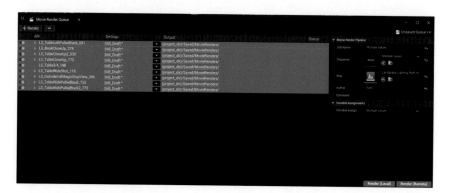

**FIGURE 12.30** MovieRenderCue.

10. It's then possible to SHIFT select the different cameras and click **Render (Local)**. The cameras and settings will then be applied to the map setup in **Movie Render Cue**.

Movie Render Cue is super powerful if you want to generate screenshots on mass with consistent visuals. It may be overkill if you are trying to share images early on in development but certainly as a project progresses, it adds consistency and settings that can be shared by all team members. This option alone will save many hours of fighting over console commands!

## Conclusion

In this chapter, we've explored a large amount of Unreals' Lighting and Post Process systems. We've looked through the project's base settings and introduced many of Unreals key workflows that help generate fantastic looking imagery in games today.

We then looked at several workflows that helped us to set up exterior lighting workflows. We focused on several different times of day to help leverage our lighting actors in different ways. After this, we looked at how we can reinforce our base/global lighting pass with additional details such as Meshes, Blueprints, VFX and more.

At the end of the chapter, we explored ways of generating images inside of Unreal combining the use of Cinematic Cameras and the HighRes shot options. The work and experience you will gain from this chapter is very much the start of the massive field of lighting. Try to keep picking different times of day and locations to help broaden your experience with lights and visual theming. For the last time in this book, we hope you enjoy the End of Chapter Quiz.

Happy world building folks!!!

## Chapter 12  Quiz

Question 1: What can we control using a Post Process Volume?

    a. Bloom.

    b. Exposure.

    c. Color Grading.

    d. All of the above.

Question 2: Why is it important to be able to light using both Physically Accurate and Artistic/Unitless Values?

    a. Studios can use either approach, so knowing what values we can leverage prepares us for different projects.

    b. We need to leverage both to make the best image.

    c. We use Physical Values to set up the main shot and artistic values to make it pretty.

Question 3: What Tool can help us place important Environment Light Actors?

    a. Environment Light Master.

    b. Environment Mixer Master.

    c. Environment Light Mixer.

Question 4: Which light is best suited to recreate sunlight?

    a. Spot light.

    b. Dominant Light.

    c. Disaster Light.

    d. Directional Light.

## Answers

Question 1: d

Question 2: a

Question 3: c

Question 4: d

# *Index*

actors 3–5
aperture 195
Attenuation Radius 181
Attributes List 131, 133
Auto Landscape Materials 149–160

Bloom 183–184, 191
block out 14–27
Blueprint Brush 119, 120, 126
Blueprint Editor 5, 145
Break Material attributes 68–70
Brush Falloff 33
brush size 33
brush type 33

Candela 182
cells 165, 167–170
chromatic aberration 184
collision radius 97
Color Grading 185
comment 50
cone angle 182
CubeGrid 15, 20–22
curl noise 114, 121–122

DCC 14
diaphragm blades 195
directional light 179, 183
dirt mask 191

edge offset 110–111, 162
emitters 4
environment light mixer 5, 183
erosion brush 35
exponential height fog 183
exposure 182–184

film grain 185
foliage 4, 88
foliage asset 89, 91
foliage mode 89

gameplay blueprints 5
global illumination 177, 185
grow in shade 98
growth 99

height control 41
hierarchical level of detail 3
HighResShot 205
hydro erosion brush 35

IES profiles 181
inclusion landscape layers 97
instances 3
inverse square falloff 181
ISO 195

landmass 119
landscape 5, 29
landscape actor 5, 32
landscape layer blend 42–43
layered landscape materials 58
landscape mode 31
landscape painting 44
landscape sculpting 32
layer blending 41
lens flare 184
Lerp 50
level blueprint 5
levels 5, 10
library 59
light mobility 180
Lightmass 177
light types 179
linear interpolate 50
loading range 171
load region 173
lumen 178
lumen light unit 182

make material attributes 48
material function 47
mesh attributes 16
mesh processing 15
model tools 15
Modeling Mode 15
movie render cue 204, 206, 208

nanite 89
Nav Meshes 7
node debug 132–133
node inspector 132–133

node palette 131
noise 161

parametric primitive creation
        tools 15
path tracer 178
PCG graph 130–131
pivots 88
point light 180
PolyGroup Edit 18–20, 23, 25
procedural foliage volume 3, 95
procedural static mesh spawner 96
profiling 6

recompile 146
Rect Light 180
reflection capture actors 7
reflections 185
roughness 47
runtime virtual texturing 72

scalability 6
sequencer 204
shutter speed 194
skeletal meshes 3
sky atmosphere 183
sky light 180, 183
slope control 40–41
smooth brush 35
specular 47
spline meshes 3

spline components 105
spline points 106
static meshes 3
statistics 6
StillRenderSetupAutomation 206
streaming 10
surface sampler 132

temperature 180, 193
terrace alpha 123
terracing 193
texture tiling 40
tiling control 46, 47, 79
tool strength 33–35
translucency 185

unitless 182
UV tools 15

variant manager 5
view modes 6
vignette 184
volumes 4, 75
volumetric cloud 183, 193

water body actors 103
water plugin 102
Weightmap 161
world building 1
world partition 5, 165
world partition editor 166

Printed in the United States
by Baker & Taylor Publisher Services